Sustainable Housing Reconstruction

Through 12 case studies from Australia, Bangladesh, Haiti, Sri Lanka, the USA and Vietnam, *Sustainable Housing Reconstruction* focuses on the housing reconstruction process after an earthquake, a tsunami, a cyclone, a flood or a fire. Design of post-disaster housing is not simply replacing the destroyed house but, as these case studies highlight, a means not only to build a safer house but also a more resilient community; not to simply return to the same condition as before the disaster, but an opportunity to build back better.

The book explores two main themes:

- Housing reconstruction is most successful when involving the users in the design and construction process.
- Housing reconstruction is most effective when it is integrated with community infrastructure, services and the means to create real livelihoods.

The case studies included in this book highlight work completed by different agencies and built environment professionals in diverse disaster-affected contexts. With a global acceleration of natural disasters, often linked to accelerating climate change, there is a critical demand for robust housing solutions for vulnerable communities.

This book provides professionals, policy-makers and community stakeholders working in the international development and disaster risk management sectors, with an evidence-based exploration of how to add real value through the design process in housing reconstruction. Herein then, the knowledge we need to build, an approach to improve our processes, a window to understanding the complex domain of post-disaster housing reconstruction.

Esther Charlesworth is Associate Professor and the Director of the Humanitarian Architecture Research Bureau (HARB) in the School of Architecture and Design, RMIT University, Melbourne, Australia. Esther is the Founding Director of Architects Without Frontiers (AWF). Her most recent book, *Humanitarian Architecture: 15 Stories of Architects Working after Disaster*, was published by Routledge in 2014.

Iftekhar Ahmed is a Research Fellow in the Humanitarian Architecture Research Bureau (HARB), School of Architecture and Design, RMIT University, Melbourne, Australia. His research interests span the areas of disaster risk reduction, climate change adaptation, urbanisation and community development.

Far too many disaster reconstruction projects regard the efficient delivery of rows of faceless houses as the measure of success. However, in this vital study Esther Charlesworth and Iftekhar Ahmed move well beyond this notion. They claim, in twelve well-chosen international case studies, that housing reconstruction can be sustainable, delivering 'added-value'. This can include newly acquired building skills that strengthen livelihoods, safety from hazard forces, community resilience and a close identification of users with their creation. The book is a joy to read, aided by a splendid layout and delightful illustrations and must qualify as the best looking book on disaster recovery ever published!

> *Ian Davis, Visiting Professor in Disaster Risk Management in Copenhagen, Lund, Kyoto and Oxford Brookes Universities*

The daunting task of rebuilding after disaster requires strong inclusion of affected people and governments, and after decades of such programmes, Esther Charlesworth and Iftekhar Ahmed have added significantly to the debate with *Sustainable Housing Reconstruction*. This detailed and colourful book is essential reading for those involved, covering a range of disasters, typologies and program approaches, putting the interests of affected people at the centre of the debate.

> *Brett Moore, Global Shelter, Infrastructure and Reconstruction Advisor, World Vision International*

Post-disaster politicians always say, 'We shall rebuild here now'. What rubbish. The disaster struck accidentally but the damage is no accident. Damaged buildings and housing are the result of hastily and poorly built structures that could not sustain the forces of nature. So, rebuilding has to be carefully thought out and well executed so there is not a repeat of the catastrophe that occurred. *Sustainable Housing Reconstruction* is a timely antidote to the rush to rebuild by laying out with cases how human and physical repair has to occur for the reconstructed post-disaster community to be fit for the future.

> *Edward J. Blakely, Honorary Professor of Urban Policy, United States Studies Centre at the University of Sydney and Director of Recovery post-Katrina for the City of New Orleans 2007–2009*

Sustainable Housing Reconstruction

Designing resilient housing after natural disasters

Esther Charlesworth and Iftekhar Ahmed

Routledge
Taylor & Francis Group

LONDON AND NEW YORK

First published 2015
by Routledge
2 Park Square, Milton Park, Abingdon, Oxon OX14 4RN

and by Routledge
711 Third Avenue, New York, NY 10017

Routledge is an imprint of the Taylor & Francis Group, an informa business

British Library Cataloguing-in-Publication Data
A catalogue record for this book is available from the British Library

Library of Congress Cataloging-in-Publication Data
Charlesworth, Esther Ruth, author.
Sustainable housing reconstruction: designing resilient housing after natural disasters / Esther Charlesworth and Iftekhar Ahmed.
pages cm
Includes bibliographical references and index.
1. Disaster victims--Housing--Case studies.
2. Ecological houses--Case studies. 3. Buildings--Repair and reconstruction--Case studies. 4. Disasters--Social aspects--Case studies. I. Ahmed, Iftekhar, 1962- author. II. Title.
HV554.5.C43 2015
363.5'83--dc23
2014034933

ISBN: 978-0-415-70260-7 (hbk)
ISBN: 978-0-415-70261-4 (pbk)
ISBN: 978-1-315-73541-2 (ebk)

Typeset in Lato
Book design, layout and typesetting by HD Design

Original Book design concept by Adrian Marshall

Cover photo by Jonas Bendiksen

Printed by Bell and Bain Ltd, Glasgow

Contents

Figures

Foreword

Introduction

Part I Overview

Part II The case studies
Bushfire | Australia

Overview

Kinglake

Marysville

Cyclone | Bangladesh

Overview

Owner-driven reconstruction

Community-based reconstruction

Earthquake | Haiti

Overview

Villa Rosa

Integrated neighbourhood approach

Foreword

Learning from the shelter sector

Graham Saunders

Head, Shelter and Settlements

International Federation of Red Cross and Red Crescent Societies

Meeting shelter needs after natural disasters, military conflicts and other crises, through the provision of emergency shelter relief and longer-term reconstruction assistance, is not a new field of endeavour. The Red Cross Red Crescent Movement archives reveal that in 1889, after the South Fork Dam burst in Pennsylvania, USA, the American Red Cross built six wooden, two-storey buildings to temporarily house those whose homes had been damaged or destroyed by the flood waters. However, some would argue that the 'business' of providing post-disaster housing has changed little since, highlighting the recent example of the large numbers of wooden 'sheds' constructed to house those rendered homeless by the 2010 earthquake in Haiti. In 2012 alone, some 32.4 million people were forced to leave their homes as a result of disasters, reflecting a steady increase on preceding years. This new caseload of people requiring shelter or housing assistance is in addition to the 100 million slum dwellers whose lives were targeted for significant improvement by 2020 as part of the Millennium Development Goals. How has the approach to addressing housing and settlement risks and vulnerabilities developed, and what have been the key lessons from what has been defined as the humanitarian shelter sector? These critical questions on how to provide effective housing solutions are explored through this innovative and timely book through looking at housing reconstruction case studies in six countries. While every case study has presented its own unique successes and challenges, Esther Charlesworth and Iftekhar Ahmed have tried to identify what are the core components of effective post-disaster housing; no easy task!

The annual economic impact of disasters has been estimated by the United Nations as totalling US$200 billion since the start of the twenty-first century, resulting from the increasing frequency of smaller and medium-scale disasters, increasing vulnerabilities through urbanisation and social and economic marginalisation, and the impacts of climate change. Following the Indian Ocean tsunami in 2004, it was estimated that nearly 50 per cent of the economic loss suffered by Indonesia was related to damage to the built environment, including housing, schools and infrastructure. Housing is a primary human need, and is often a household's most valuable asset. Quantifying the scale of the humanitarian shelter sector and the housing needs resulting from disasters and crises is a challenge. It is interesting to note that 75 per cent of the disaster response activities of the 189 National Red Cross and Red Crescent Societies (excluding health and food security emergencies) included the provision of housing assistance to affected populations. The scale of need remains significant, as disasters in recent years have highlighted. The extensive flooding in Asia in 2007 resulted in the homes of more than 60 million people being damaged or destroyed, the 2010 floods in Pakistan destroyed 1.6 million homes, and over 1 million homes in the Philippines were damaged or destroyed by the typhoon that struck in late 2013. Population displacement as a result of conflict and civil unrest leads to the need for both short- and longer term housing assistance, with over 2 million households displaced as a result of the crisis in Syria, 250,000 in the Central African Republic and 100,000 in South Sudan in early 2014. However, the financial and material resources to assist the households affected by such disasters, from both the affected governments themselves and the international donors, can meet only some of these needs.

For the majority of people, outside of a disaster or conflict, ensuring adequate or appropriate housing is an iterative process over time. The house may have been inherited, and adapted through repair or extension. Alternatively, the property or land may have been purchased, with a loan, with cash, or through exchange, or constructed by the household themselves with their own labour or through the formal or informal engagement of others. Accommodation may be owned, or rented, may be substantially constructed and durable or of simple construction to enable rapid adaptation or relocation. Such processes are informed by local housing typologies and building technologies, forms of tenure for both land and property, social and familial norms, and the economic and financial systems used by the respective community. In the recovery and reconstruction phase following a major disaster, typically when the scale of both national and international assistance decreases, these processes are re-established over time as the affected community strives to return to normality. However, in the aftermath of disaster, particularly a rapid onset emergency such as an earthquake, a hurricane, a landslide or sudden flooding, humanitarian shelter interventions typically ignore or inhibit such processes through external supply or product-driven activities, such as the provision of tents or other forms of prefabricated temporary housing. Although consideration is often given to cultural concerns and the use of locally sourced labour, such approaches typically do not fully capitalise on existing housing processes. Perhaps of greater consequence are the potential economic benefits that this book explores, such as investment in livelihood opportunities that could enable the affected community to recover from the disaster,

MEETING LOCAL NEEDS: An IFRC-supported community rain water tank in Bangladesh.

and increased knowledge and understanding of the housing and settlement risks that need to be addressed to reduce the future vulnerability of both people and property. All the examples in this book show how well-programmed post-disaster reconstruction activities have economically benefited local businesses and construction workers, as well as building local capacity and reducing disaster risk through building resilient housing.

The provision of rapid emergency housing assistance has significantly improved over the last decade, through improved coordination, the advances in the quality and consistency of shelter relief items, including plastic sheeting and tents, and the provision of standardised housing kits, tools, materials and cash to enable self-recovery by affected households. There is also far greater recognition of the need to identify and address key housing and settlement risks and vulnerabilities from the outset of a response, through informed relief interventions and the inclusion of awareness-raising activities or training as part of the on going programming. However, the widely varying standard and scope of both interim and longer term housing assistance in Haiti following the 2010 earthquake, in Pakistan following the 2010 and 2011 floods, and other major disasters, highlight how much more work

is to be done at both the programmatic level but crucially at the institutional level. Some of the case studies in this book, particularly from Haiti and Australia, show an emerging recognition of the link between short- and long-term housing, a pointer to dealing with this crucial challenge.

Key challenges for both strategic decision-makers and practitioners in addressing post-disaster housing needs include defining the most appropriate interventions addressing the risks and vulnerabilities, and understanding the technical and regulatory environment to ensure the rapid and equitable provision of assistance. Government ministries and local authority offices often do include personnel with relevant backgrounds in the built environment, but in these times of lean central government and an increasing reliance on the contracting-in of expertise and capacity when required, the in-house specialist know-how is not necessarily readily available. Similarly, many humanitarian shelter agencies lack dedicated specialists who can address these issues, which has resulted in poor-quality programming, inadequate housing solutions or conflict with the regulatory authorities.

It is alarming to note that not all the major international non-governmental organisations which implement large-scale housing and reconstruction activities have in-house technical expertise with a background in the built environment. Indeed, several agencies that are household names lack even a single in-house technical adviser to inform agency decision-making, let alone ensuring quality assurance at country level. While acknowledging that technical expertise alone is not sufficient, and that the disaster context in particular requires addressing both 'hard' and 'soft' needs, the lack of such input clearly results in less-informed decision-making. It is commonly recognised among humanitarian shelter practitioners that the shelter sector itself remains poorly understood and under-represented among international agencies' core competencies and donor priorities, inhibiting investment in such dedicated in-house technical competencies. Such an investment can result in a well-managed and technically sound solution, but given the complexities and often conflicting variables in the post-disaster context, this limits the iterative development of better practice and sector learning. Of course, in the majority of contexts, there is no lack of technical knowledge and capacity in the form of architects, engineers, planners, building technicians and individuals with specialist building skills. These individuals are typically working in the private sector, on an individual basis or as part of a commercial enterprise, and may be contracted as part of the relief and reconstruction activities. The challenge is that, typically but not always, such individuals do not have the required experience of the post-disaster context or of working methodologies that require the active participation of the affected household, incremental construction, community-led oversight processes, etc. This is particularly the case for professionals trained or working in well-developed and less disaster-prone countries, but is also an issue in other contexts

where individuals with professional qualifications are rarely involved in individual, low-income household construction in either urban or rural contexts. It is therefore encouraging to note that most of the case studies here have highlighted the significant role that can be played by built environment professionals, perhaps a hopeful signal that a future expansion of such a role is in the offing.

Perhaps of more major, long-term concern is the lack of adequate recognition, among humanitarian actors and decision-makers, of the built environment as a sector in its own right. Built environment or settlement issues in the humanitarian field are typically separated into 'housing', 'water and sanitation', 'infrastructure', 'urban risk', and so on, whereas for technical professionals, be they architects, planners, municipal officials or managers, these issues are all components of the built environment. This lack of a common, settlement approach to post-disaster relief and reconstruction impedes the development of durable, comprehensive response strategies and continuity with ongoing housing development. Therefore the selection of the case studies in this book must be complimented as they all reflect a wider gamut of interventions as part of an 'integrated' process of reconstruction of the built environment, not the mere rebuilding of houses to replace those damaged by disaster.

Meeting post-disaster housing needs and ensuring sustainable, resilient housing reconstruction for vulnerable households, must be the goal for governments, the humanitarian shelter sector and the at-risk populations themselves. Continuing to learn from the field, and to engage all of these entities in advancing the practice and policy of achieving this goal, still remains a major challenge.

This book points the way to addressing that challenge.

TECHNICAL ADVICE: IFRC supervision helps to ensure appropriate housing reconstruction in Haiti.

Acknowledgements

In the course of writing this book – over nearly three years – many people from around the globe have kindly contributed to this project despite their profound loss after disaster. The sharing of their experiences of the post-disaster rebuilding process deserves our full gratitude.

We would like to thank all the disaster-affected communities who have generously welcomed us, people who opened their doors to us, and who spoke unreservedly of rebuilding their lives and housing.

Among the many professionals and agency staff who helped us in our research, we would like to thank Graham Saunders, Ken Alexander, Selvadurai Arumainathan, Bob Bairstow, Amanda Bauman, Nguyen Thanh Binh, Guillaume Chantry, Britt Christiaens, Nancy Doran, Adith Shah Durjoy, John Fien, Emilie Forestier, Ibralebbe Abdul Hameed, Phan Duc Hanh, Piyal Ganepola, Max Ginn, Kushil Gunasekara, Peter Johns, Khondaker Hasibul Kabir, Cai Trung Nhu, Emmanuel Pajot, Jim Pate, David Perkes, Colin Price, Paskuwalhandi Sampath, Mannan Ali Shaikh, Henri Markus Stalder, Chris Stanley, Le Tuan Thang, Pham Thi Thien Tro, Noll Tufani, Aziza Usoof and Anna Wachtmeister. Also gracious thanks are due to those who served valuably as interpreters, including Phan Duc Hanh, Calvens Joseph and Bertram Pereira.

We would like to thank the Australian Research Council for funding the field research on the selected housing case studies. We would also like to express our sincere gratitude to Fran Ford and Alanna Donaldson at Routledge for guiding this book from an idea through to final publication. We would not have completed the project without Adrian Marshall, whose expert and diligent editing and graphic skills have refined the language, sharpened our arguments and given the book its final shape. Thanks also to Kate Ryle for the drawings that illustrate the case study projects.

Finally, we would like to thank our respective families for their encouragement, advice and patience that saw this book through to publication.

Introduction

More than a roof overhead: Post-disaster housing reconstruction to enable resilient communities

'It's sad to say, but then again nothing but the truth that all these facilities and development emerged from a tragic disaster and we would never have been able to change the landscape of the villages with such creations of housing complexes and everything else if not for the waves of compassion that overpowered the waves of destruction!'

– Kushil Gunasekara, Founder, Foundation of Goodness, Sri Lanka

SAFER: Post-disaster housing in Vietnam 'built back better' than before. Source: Tuan Tran Anh.

This book, *Sustainable Housing Reconstruction: Designing resilient housing after natural disasters*, analyses emerging approaches to designing and constructing resilient housing after natural disasters. As the title suggests, post-disaster housing reconstruction is not only the replacement of the damaged house, but also an attempt to build a safer house; not to simply return to the same condition as before the disaster, but an opportunity to build more resilient housing and thereby address the vulnerabilities that allowed damage to occur in the first place. The now popular concept of 'building back better'[1] after an earthquake, a tsunami, a typhoon, a flood or a fire, runs throughout the book: how long-term development objectives can be addressed early in the shelter reconstruction process, together with the importance of building-in disaster risk reduction measures in the original housing design. A second key theme is the role of built environment professionals, such as architects, in supporting the complex process undertaken by a maze of key stakeholders in any reconstruction project. The book follows on from key concepts introduced in Esther Charlesworth's book, Humanitarian Architecture,[2] including the discourses and design practices that have recently emerged in the field of 'emergency' or 'humanitarian' architecture.

The increasingly frequent and massive disasters in recent history have been accompanied by large and extensive reconstruction programs instigated by a plethora of agencies worldwide, which in turn have been followed by extensive evaluations and critiques of these efforts. Notwithstanding the objectivity of such critiques and their intent to highlight what is often lacking, they have also focused on problems rather than solutions for post-disaster housing. This book has therefore looked for effective rather than exemplar housing reconstruction case studies which may inform future practice in the shelter field.

In exploring what actually constitutes 'sustainable housing reconstruction', this book examines the successes, and also challenges, of 12 housing reconstruction programs in Australia, Bangladesh, Haiti, Sri Lanka, the USA and Vietnam, all built after natural disasters in the last decade. A significant amount of field research has sharpened the selection of case studies included in this book to show a global picture of effectiveness in the post-disaster housing reconstruction field.

Many key issues have continually emerged throughout the case studies. Housing reconstruction is not only about building new houses but about integrating a range of community infrastructure and services to reconstruct a habitable and safe built environment. Housing reconstruction,

we have learnt, is also an opportunity to build local capacities and economies by training built environment professionals to contribute to humanitarian architecture and, importantly, building community resilience in an uncertain world of unfolding climate change and magnified future disasters.

TEAMWORK: Many people's skills contribute to a house being rebuilt in Marysville after the Black Saturday bushfires.

A key message learnt from all 12 case studies is the importance of multi-disciplinary teamwork in which built environment professionals work together with government and development agencies, and importantly, with disaster-affected communities themselves, to achieve more than just a roof overhead – to provide shelter that provides safety and potentially a means to improve livelihood and human well-being.

Notes

1 IFRC, *Annual Report 2008* (Geneva: IFRC, International Federation of Red Cross and Red Crescent Societies, 2008). The slogan 'building back better', originally coined by former President of the USA, Bill Clinton, in the aftermath of the 2004 Indian Ocean tsunami is now widely used by humanitarian and other agencies in the post-disaster reconstruction context, indicative of the recognition of the need to build safer houses that protect their residents from future disasters.

2 Charlesworth, E., *Humanitarian Architecture. Fifteen Stories of Architects Working after Disaster* (London: Routledge, 2014).

PART I
Overview

Achievements in housing reconstruction despite mounting odds

Humanitarian agencies and professionals are often presented with extremely challenging circumstances after a disaster. Their reconstruction tasks are complex – managing the range of stakeholders involved, and the severe displacement, suffering and trauma of the disaster victims. These challenges continue to mount as rapid and unplanned urbanisation, environmental degradation and climate change proceed unabated globally.[1] Examples of effective reconstruction practice are understandably hard to find in such a scenario. When rebuilding projects achieve sustainable outcomes, that is, where communities and not just buildings are rebuilt, where infrastructure needs are considered at the same time as housing needs, when owners can genuinely input into the design of their homes – these are the sort of projects that can offer valuable lessons for action following future disasters. The case studies presented in this book have been selected because, across the wide range of their achievements and stakeholders, they have demonstrated their grasp of the complexities of housing reconstruction and their effectiveness in approaching the problems in an innovative, cross-disciplinary way to build physical and social resilience. They are based on narratives of beneficiary communities, built environment professionals, and humanitarian and other agency staff, supplemented by the observations of the authors.

Asia experiences the greatest disaster impacts globally[2] and three of the six countries covered here are from Asia: Bangladesh, Sri Lanka and Vietnam. In the extreme poverty of Haiti, an earthquake dealt a severe blow to an already vulnerable nation. Economically stronger countries are not spared, and two such case study countries that have experienced severe disasters have been included: Australia and the USA.

The key features of the case studies include:

Australia: Supported by the State Government of Victoria, temporary and then permanent housing was successfully developed after the 2009 Black Saturday bushfires in the devastated towns of Kinglake and Marysville.

Bangladesh: After Cyclone Aila in 2009, an owner-driven project was implemented by the Bangladesh Red Crescent Society in Khulna district and, second, a community-based project led by a team of architects was built in Satkhira District.

RANGE OF STAKEHOLDERS: Even children contribute to the reconstruction task in Bangladesh.

Haiti: In the dense, informal settlements of Port-au-Prince devastated by the 2010 earthquake, Cordaid and its partners implemented a community development program. The second case study presents the International Federation of Red Cross and Red Crescent Societies' 'integrated neighbourhood approach' where community infrastructure was incorporated with housing reconstruction.

Sri Lanka: After the 2004 Indian Ocean tsunami, the Foundation of Goodness undertook a resettlement program in Seenigama on the southern coast, as part of a long-term community development initiative. The second case study focuses on an owner-driven project in Tissamaharama, led by UN-Habitat.

The USA: Hurricane Katrina in 2005 catalysed a participative reconstruction program led by the architects of the Gulf Coast Community Design Studio in Biloxi, Mississippi. In New Orleans, Louisiana, Habitat for Humanity built a Musicians' Village to resettle the musicians of this city with a strong musical heritage.

Vietnam: Development Workshop France promoted disaster-resilient housing in Hue through its reconstruction projects after Typhoons Xangsane (2006) and Ketsana (2009), and child-friendly reconstruction was led by Save the Children UK in Danang after Typhoon Xangsane, 2006.

Notes

1   Jha, A. *et al.*, *Safer Homes, Stronger Communities: A Handbook for Reconstructing after Natural Disasters* (Washington, DC: World Bank, 2013).

2   EM-DAT (2013) *The International Disaster Database.* Available at: http://imgur.com/a/KdyTV#0 (accessed 15 April 2014).

COMPLEX TASKS: Rebuilding after a massive earthquake in Haiti. ▷

PART II
The case studies

BANGLADESH

VIETNAM

SRI LANKA

AUSTRALIA

Bushfire | Australia

Twelve years of drought, compounded by a severe heatwave, led to the bushfires that struck the state of Victoria, Australia, on 7 February, 2009.[1, 2] In the 'Black Saturday bushfires', the worst bushfires in the nation's history, 173 people died, and more than 2,300 houses were destroyed, displacing more than 7,500 people.[3]

In its investigation of the bushfires, the 2009 Victorian Bushfires Royal Commission reported:

'The most serious consequence of the fires was the death of 173 people. Left behind are families, friends and communities still trying to come to terms with their loss. Accompanying this loss of life is the fires' impact on property and the infrastructure that supports communities, as well as the substantial environmental impact, which will take years to fully reveal itself – let alone be ameliorated.'[4]

The towns of Kinglake and Marysville experienced the full impact of Black Saturday and required the most significant reconstruction efforts. In both towns, the transition from emergency to recovery – from short-term temporary accommodation to long-term permanent housing – demonstrates a model reconstruction process.

Black Saturday prompted the revision of, and mandatory compliance with, building standards and regulations to ensure better housing resistance to future bushfires.[5] The Building Commission of Victoria produced a number of guidebooks to assist disaster-affected communities to retrofit or rebuild safer houses according to the new standards.[6]

The Australian Institute of Architects (Victoria) and the Office of the Victorian Government Architect initiated the 'Bushfire Homes Service': 19 architectural firms provided innovative house designs on a pro bono basis following the new revised building standards.[7] Although these designs were considered generally too expensive by bushfire-affected communities and never really implemented, this initiative still demonstrates the potential of architects to contribute to post-disaster reconstruction.

The Victorian Bushfire Reconstruction and Recovery Authority (VBRRA), formed after Black Saturday, gathered together professionals with relevant skills from different government departments. A VBRRA-organised competition invited teams of builders and architects to submit tenders for the design and construction of demonstration houses that complied with the standards and regulations required to resist a high level of bushfire attack.[8] Two winning designs were built, one in Kinglake and the other in Marysville. The Marysville house remained an isolated example, but the Kinglake house was replicated, resulting in 14 such houses.

The 'Re-Growth Pod Competition' organised by 1:1 Architects (now Edwards Moore) invited designs for houses in bushfire-prone areas that are built around an existing concrete module or 'pod'. Though the winning designs remain unbuilt, the pod installed after Black Saturday houses a bushfire-affected household, and is discussed in the Kinglake case study that follows.

A key reconstruction project, though not housing, is the Narbethong Community Hall, built after Black Saturday in a fire-devastated area. Designed and built in collaboration between Emergency Architects Australia, BVN Architecture, Arup and a number of other consulting firms, this building plays a central role in the bushfire-affected community in Narbethong, particularly in its post-bushfire recovery process. Because it is built to withstand a high level of bushfire attack, the building also offers a safe refuge to the community.

Most housing design and construction in Australia is generally undertaken by builders or homeowners themselves, and architects have a lesser role in the housing sector. This is reflected in the limited uptake of the above architectural designs developed after Black Saturday. Nevertheless, the following case studies show the contributions of architects and built environment professionals in post-bushfire housing reconstruction, particularly in designing temporary villages.

◁ **AFTERMATH:** Marysville soon after the bushfire. Source: Barry Thomas.

Black Saturday bushfires, 2009

Linking temporary and permanent housing, Kinglake

Kinglake, with a population of about 1000 before the Black Saturday bushfires, is a small town at an elevation of 550 metres.[9] On 7 February 2009, power lines north of Kinglake collapsed in strong winds and ignited open grassland made dry in the hot season and by a preceding heatwave. The fire travelled rapidly, sweeping through Kinglake and its surrounding areas, causing massive devastation. The Kinglake area experienced the full impact of the Black Saturday bushfires, with 120 people killed and more than 1,200 houses and many commercial buildings completely destroyed.[10, 11]

The Victorian and Federal governments responded quickly, together with community organisations, setting up relief centres and providing emergency accommodation. Then the task of reconstruction commenced, starting with the construction of a temporary village while the long-term rebuilding of permanent housing progressed.

Map of Victoria, Australia showing location of Kinglake.

KINGLAKE

'The bushfire was a harrowing experience. My house burnt down along with other houses on this street. There were thirty houses here and after the fire there were only three left.'

– Anthony Smith, Kinglake

FORESTED: Kinglake and the hills of the Kinglake Range.

Implementing agencies
Temporary village implemented by VBRRA
Permanent housing built by homeowners with some support from VBRRA

Donors
Government of Victoria. Some products and services provided by: BlueScope Steel; Bosch; IKEA; LSA Hospital; Fleetwood; FMG

Context
Black Saturday bushfires, 2009

Location
Kinglake, Victoria, Australia

Number of houses built
Temporary village: 18 one-bedroom cottages and 38 two-bedroom cottages; 20 single persons quarters. Total 76 units

Cost
US$7.4 million for four temporary villages
Temporary village cottages approximately US$33,000–40,000
Permanent houses as per homeowners' budgets

Type of post-disaster project
Staged reconstruction from temporary to permanent housing

Date completed
Temporary village built 2009
Permanent housing approximately 90 per cent complete by 2013

Why this project case study?

Bushfires are a major hazard in Australia, and Kinglake was the area most severely impacted by the worst bushfire in Australian history. The Kinglake housing reconstruction, starting from a temporary village and leading in the long-term to permanent housing, demonstrates a model process of transition from emergency to recovery. At the same time, the example of the Re-Growth Pod discussed below provides a note of caution on the sole use of prefabricated design solutions as a temporary housing solution.

Agency roles

Three days after Black Saturday, the Victorian Bushfire Reconstruction and Recovery Authority (VBRRA) was established by the Victorian and Federal governments, and among other achievements managed the construction, operation and transition of four temporary villages, including one at Kinglake. A key partner, the government's Department of Human Services (DHS) allocated and managed the temporary housing.[12] The site plan of Kinglake temporary village was designed by a pro bono consortium of architects (Architectus Group, Antarctica, ARG Architects, Butterpaper Architecture and Emergency Architects) under the banner of Emergency Architects Australia Joint Venture (EAA JV).

Numerous organisations donated products and services to the temporary village, including Fortescue Metals Group (FMG) and Fleetwood (single person's quarters, called 'dongas'), BlueScope Steel (dining hall and storage sheds), IKEA (kitchen units), Lort Smith Animal Hospital (fences for pet-holding areas), Bosch (domestic appliances), Linfox and the Salvation Army (household items).[13]

The Bushfire Appeal Fund, initiated by the State and Federal governments and the Australian Red Cross and administered by DHS, provided emergency, rebuilding and social support funding to the bushfire-affected communities.[14] Funding to affected households varied according to the extent of housing damage, specific household needs, whether the house was insured and other factors. In most cases, this funding assisted in the reconstruction of permanent housing.

Max Ginn

Assistant Director, Asset Planning Services, DHS, Melbourne (Seconded to VBRRA as Rebuilding Advisory Service Manager)

....

'I'm an architect by background, working in the housing and building side of DHS. After Black Saturday, like many other people from the government, I was appointed to work in the newly formed VBRRA. I was responsible for overseeing rebuilding of housing in all the areas affected by the Black Saturday bushfires, including Kinglake and Marysville.

'When we proposed the Kinglake temporary village, the local community was not convinced of its need. However, once construction started, they changed their mind and many people said later that it helped hold their community together.

'In conjunction with the villages, we organised a design competition for a model house, inviting teams of architects and builders to participate. We built the winning designs in Kinglake and Marysville, which are now public housing. Some people followed the design in Kinglake. But the main aim was to demonstrate that it is possible to build an affordable house with a high bushfire attack level in accordance with the new building regulations. Our Rebuilding Advisers were very successful in helping many to do that.'

Peter Johns

Architect, Butterpaper Architecture, Melbourne

....

'It was a great experience working in a team of architects from different firms. We wanted the temporary village to be connected to Kinglake town through sight lines defined by a central circulation spine. We didn't want the place to become isolated like a ghetto.

'The cottage plots were on a suburban scale with reasonably-sized front and back yards; these were people used to living on large land, so privacy was important. Each cottage could be accessed by car with parking next to the front porch so that people could enter without getting their shoes muddy. Although the site was connected to the town, it was designed to get more private as one goes further in.

'Trees on the edges of the site meant that the housing and other buildings had to be set back by 25 metres to avoid fire risk. An existing pond on the site was fenced off for safety, especially for children.'

The reconstruction process

US$7.4 million was provided by the government for building, running and eventually closing four temporary villages in Victoria, including the one in Kinglake, over a four-year period. At the same time, the government-led 'Bushfire Appeal Fund' supported households to initiate the permanent housing reconstruction process.

The temporary village was built in the centre of Kinglake on private farming land leased by DHS through the local council. VBRRA managed the construction, including laying-out basic infrastructure and utility services, using volunteer groups and builders, including architects from the EAA JV. DHS's Office of Housing provided one and two bedroom cottages from its existing stock. Known as 'granny flats', such cottages are usually provided as social housing for elderly, disabled or young family members who want a separate residence on existing family property.[15] FMG and Fleetwood provided 'dongas' – four-person accommodation for single people – from stock from Western Australian mining sites.

Other facilities, including a community dining hall, storage shed for residents' belongings, pet-holding area and children's playground, were built. A Rebuilding Advisory Centre (RAC) building was designed pro bono by Bamford-Dash Architects, Melbourne. Architecture students from Monash University (Caulfield, Victoria) also designed and built a community pavilion with barbeque facilities.

Construction of the temporary village began in May 2009 and was completed in September 2009. In July 2009, residents began moving in. A Rebuilding Advisory Service (RAS) was provided by VBRRA and four qualified Rebuilding Advisers appointed (two each based in Kinglake and Marysville) to provide advice and help on a range of reconstruction issues such as the clearing of bushfire-devastated properties, financing, planning and building approvals, design and construction, contracts and insurance.

The temporary village was closed in late 2012 and the housing units were returned to the Office of Housing, DHS, the dongas (except one) were collected by their donors and the land was returned to the farmer. A portion of the land with the RAC, community dining hall, storage shed, manager's office and one donga was acquired by the local council and adapted for other uses. The RAC was converted into a Parks Victoria visitors' centre and part of it was leased to a non-profit organisation, Workspace Australia. The storage shed is used by Parks Victoria as a workshop and storeroom.

Key project features and design aspects

Housing

The temporary housing consisted mainly of 'granny flats'; 18 one-bedroom and 38 two-bedroom cottages, about 42 square metres and 50 square metres in size respectively. The two-bedroom housing was an elongated version of the one-bedroom housing, with the extra bedroom added at one end. Each cottage had an entry porch at the front, leading to a living room with kitchen, connected to the bedroom, or bedrooms, and a bathroom. The units were placed on, and attached to, concrete footings and raised on a 1-metre plinth. The walls consisted of pine wood framing with exterior and interior fibre cement cladding with insulation between. The roofing was of timber framing, steel sheet exterior cladding and fibre cement ceiling. Each unit had a fenced rear yard for the safety of children and pets.

Additional housing in the temporary village was provided for 20 single persons in five dongas, each accommodating four persons in separate rooms. Altogether there were 76 dwelling units in the temporary village.

STUDENT-LED: The community barbeque pavilion in the temporary village, designed and built by Monash University architecture students. Source: Peter Johns.

CENTRAL: The children's playground set at the heart of the Kinglake temporary village. Source: Peter Johns.

WELL-SITED: Aerial view and site plan of the Kinglake temporary village. Source: aerial view: Peter Johns

Site layout

The site plan consisted of a public zone at the entry to the site, where all the community facilities were built, and behind which a private housing zone was located. A central circulation spine connected the site to the main street of Kinglake and at the other end to an area planned for a bushfire memorial (eventually not built). A children's playground was located at the centre of the site as a focal point. Each cottage had vehicular access and front and back yards comparable to housing plots in suburban subdivisions.

Community facilities

The main community facilities in the temporary village consisted of: a dining hall with six kitchens; a storage shed with lockers for personal belongings and valuable household items; a community pavilion with barbeque; a children's playground; communal toilets, showers, washing machines and dryers; fenced areas to exercise 'off-leash' pets; and a manager's office and residence.

1. Site entry
2. Rebuilding Advisory Centre
3. Dongas arranged around a central space
4. Central circulation spine
5. Community barbeque pavilion
6. Children's playground
7. Communal dining hall
8. Community showers and laundry
9. Water Tanks

In a 'shelter' for five years

Jacqueline Marchant, a beauty therapist, lived with her partner Stoney Black, a construction worker, and her son David, in a 'Re-Growth Pod' in Kinglake West, an area close to the town of Kinglake, after their house was destroyed in the Black Saturday bushfires. The 'pod' developed by 1:1 Architects (now Edwards Moore) is a prefabricated concrete structure designed to serve as a post-disaster shelter and it was expected that a larger house would be built around it over time. The pod was donated by 1:1 Architects and was brought on a truck and installed on the site. A design competition was organised by the architects, inviting proposals for using the pod as a basis for building a larger house.

Jacqueline and her partner did not follow the winning design and instead chose to start building their new house as a separate structure. Facing the difficult circumstances of organising the resources to build a new house, the household stayed in the pod for almost five years. Over time, they grew weary; according to Jacqueline, the lack of ventilation and light made living in it difficult. She mentioned that concrete, being a porous material and absorbing moisture, made the pod very cold in the winter. Architects Ben Edwards and Juliet Moore argue that the pod is not designed for long-term living, but rather to provide temporary shelter on a homeowner's site, removing the need to relocate to temporary accommodation elsewhere, and allowing the household to gradually reconstruct its house around it.

Jacqueline and her partner did make some additions to make the pod more liveable. A concrete porch was paved in the front; a double-glazed door was attached to the front wall for privacy and to keep out rain; a metal sheet structure was built around the toilet and washing area and included a laundry inside. When asked how she benefited from the pod, Jacqueline said. 'It's shelter, that's good about it.'

Clockwise from above – Jacqueline Marchant; the Re-Growth Pod being craned in; installed; (source: Ben Edwards and Juliet Moore) and after five years; and design drawings for the Re-Growth Pod.

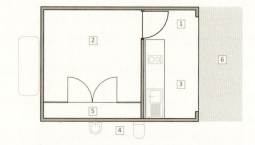

0   5   1   2M

GROUND FLOOR
1. Entry
2. Bedroom
3. Kitchen
4. Toilet
5. Cupboard
6. Porch

Temporary village was 'fantastic'

Greg Rogers is a tattoo artist in Kinglake. Before Black Saturday, he lived with his partner in a house built in the 1930s, and in the bushfire the house was completely burnt down. They had no early warning and barely managed to escape with their lives. Greg and his partner stayed at the house of a friend of his partner, but a year later they separated and Greg moved out. He found a two-bedroom cottage at the temporary village and stayed there for 18 months with his daughter. He could not afford to build a new house, so now he rents a small unit in town.

Greg is very happy with the time he spent at the temporary village. He developed epilepsy after the bushfire, but in the temporary village he felt secure because he had people around him. He made new friends and enjoyed the various events at the village such as Christmas celebrations, community dinners and barbeques. 'I can't complain about anything there. I think it was fantastic; it really helped me out,' he says.

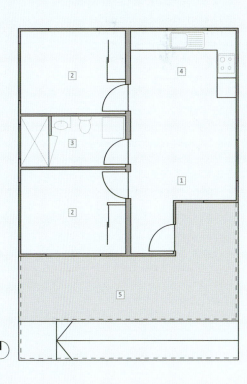

Greg Rogers; a floor plan of a two-bedroom cottage at the temporary village. Source: floor plan adapted from Max Ginn.

Success factors

Sensitivity of design

Instead of developing the temporary village as only a short-term facility and designing it in a regimental barrack-type layout (as is often the case in such post-disaster emergency housing), special attention was given to the specific site conditions and needs of the residents. A radial layout with a central spine allowed public and private zones to be defined, as well as creating a central community space marked by the children's playground.

The community dining hall in this development provided a space for entertaining guests, and kitchens created the opportunity for communal cooking and socialising, as well as providing cooking facilities for the single residents of the dongas. The range of facilities – storage shed, children's playground, pet-holding area, central location with access to schools and other amenities – helped residents to function as a 'normal' community despite the great impact and trauma caused by the bushfire.

In addition to site planning, the architects provided design advice at a more detailed level. The five dongas were arranged around a central space with a timber deck to serve as a focal point; a fabric shade sail over this space defined it further as a comfortable community area. Cottage porches were designed as outdoor decks with railings, and served not only as entry points, but also as semi-public open space for residents. Such details enhanced the carefully laid-out village, making it liveable for an extended period of more than three years.

Interim solution

While in the short term, bushfire-affected people could stay with relatives and friends, the temporary village provided a medium-term solution to the housing shortage caused by the bulk of the housing in Kinglake being destroyed by the bushfire.

Community cohesion

The temporary village helped to maintain a sense of community for the residents. It allowed them to remain close to their previous place of residence and to maintain their social networks. Relocating the affected residents away from Kinglake would have delayed long-term recovery by disrupting community links

Linkage between temporary and permanent housing

The temporary village allowed residents to be close to their destroyed homes and helped them initiate and undertake reconstruction of permanent housing. Residents could work on reconstruction during the day and easily return to the village to rest for the night.

The Rebuilding Advisory Service (RAS)

The RAS, established by VBRRA in 2010 and operated from the RAC in Kinglake, was instrumental in facilitating the reconstruction of permanent housing. Many of the affected people had no previous experience in building a house, and the RAS supported them at a time of great disruption and trauma. Face-to-face consultations and on-site advice and sharing of knowledge from the RAS central information repository eased the transition from temporary to permanent housing.

Voluntary contributions

Pro bono services provided by the EAA JV made a significant qualitative impact on the site plan of the temporary village. Again, architecture students from Monash University volunteered to design and build the community pavilion and contributed to the quality of community life at the temporary village, at the same time gaining valuable experience for future work in the post-disaster reconstruction field.

| DESTRUCTION: A resident at the remains of his house. Source: Terry and Sharon Donovan.

Black Saturday bushfires, 2009

Linking temporary and permanent housing, Marysville

The town of Marysville, with a population of 500 people, is a popular tourist destination in the State of Victoria. On the early afternoon of 7 February 2009, the 'Murrindindi Mill Fire' started near a sawmill in the town of Murrindindi, north-west of Marysville. The fire burned rapidly, aided by strong wind, and devastated Marysville and its surrounding areas, killing 34 people and destroying nearly 600 houses and many commercial buildings. The town centre was destroyed, as were Marysville's public facilities, including the police station, the primary school, the kindergarten and the health clinic. [16, 17] As in Kinglake, following extensive emergency response operations, a temporary village was built as an interim solution and as part of the initial stage of transition to long-term permanent housing. The project re-established the settlement and reconstructed housing.

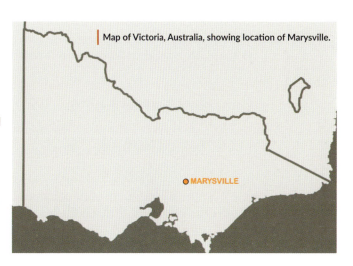

| Map of Victoria, Australia, showing location of Marysville.

MARYSVILLE

'I wanted to defend my house, but it became pitch-black with smoke and the electricity and water supply stopped. I escaped just in time before the whole house burnt down.'

– Terry Donovan, Marysville

FUTURE PROMISE: Temporary village housing (later used as school camp buildings).

Implementing agencies
**Temporary Village implemented by VBRRA
Permanent housing built by homeowners with
some support from VBRRA**

Donors
**Government of Victoria. Some products and
services provided by: BlueScope Steel; Bosch;
IKEA; LSA Hospital; Fleetwood; FMG**

Context
Black Saturday bushfires, 2009

Location
Marysville, Victoria, Australia

Number of houses built
**Temporary Village: 10 one-bedroom cottages
and 40 two-bedroom cottages; 1 three-bedroom
house; 3 four-bedroom houses; 16 single persons
quarters. Total 94 units**

Cost
**US$7.4 million for four temporary villages
Temporary village cottages US$33,000–40,000
depending on size
Permanent houses as per homeowners' budgets**

Type of post-disaster project
**Staged reconstruction from temporary to
permanent housing**

Date completed
**Temporary village built 2009
Permanent housing approximately 90 per cent
complete by 2013**

Why this project case study?

After Kinglake, Marysville was the area most affected by the Black Saturday bushfires. As was the case in Kinglake, the transition from temporary to permanent housing in Marysville was successfully achieved. In addition, the adaptive reuse of the Marysville Temporary Village, beyond the emergency stage, is an example of effective long-term utilisation of reconstruction infrastructure.

Agency roles

The government agencies and donors were the same at Marysville as they were at Kinglake, and performed very similar roles, though a different pro bono architectural firm, Splinter Society, designed the site plan for the temporary village in Marysville, and two other Rebuilding Advisers operated from the Rebuilding Advisory Service (RAS) centre in Marysville.

The reconstruction process

The reconstruction process was similar to the one followed in Kinglake, where the same models of cottages and 'dongas' were used. In Marysville, the local council leased land, about 2 kilometres from the town centre, from the Ecumenical

Society of Australia (ESA). The land was previously a camping site and had been impacted by the bushfire. The site plan was designed pro bono by Splinter Society, an architectural firm in Melbourne, and VBRRA managed the construction, including laying out basic infrastructure and utility services, using volunteer groups and builders, and including services from FMG and J&M Bailey. A local individual donated one three-bedroom house, and three four-bedroom houses were acquired by VBRRA. Other facilities, including a community dining hall, a storage shed for residents' belongings, a tools library, a pet-holding area and a children's playground were built. The temporary village was completed by early July 2009, though residents had started moving in from mid-May 2009.

As in Kinglake, staying at the temporary village made it easier for residents to plan and design the rebuilding of their devastated housing. Similarly, they were supported in this process by the RAS, a specific building for which was built in central Marysville, following the Kinglake design provided pro bono by Bamford-Dash Architects, Melbourne.

The temporary village was closed in late 2012 and then acquired by the Outdoor Education Group and renamed as Camp Marysville to serve as a school camping site. The dongas were collected by their donors. Forty-one cottages and the community structures were kept on site and adapted for use in the school camp.

Chris Stanley

Architect, Splinter Society,
Melbourne

'I gave a lot of pro bono time and effort in designing the site plan for the Marysville Temporary Village. Our office had a good relationship with DHS; they were very supportive of our design ideas.

The design was based on the site conditions of the undulating land and the many trees remaining on it. All the trees were kept and the cottages were laid out around them.

I wanted to create more of a village, not a suburban layout. Cars were kept out of the site with parking provided on the edge. A network of footpaths allowed connection and communication within the community. The cottages were laid out in a staggered pattern so that each cottage had an open view instead of looking onto the neighbours.'

Ken Alexander

Rebuilding Adviser,
Marysville

'I have worked in the building industry for 40 years, as a subcontractor and builder, also with DHS on urban upgrade projects. After the bushfires I was appointed as a Rebuilding Adviser, alternating between Marysville and Gippsland as required.

My role was to advise the bushfire victims on how best to fast track the building process, resolving difficulties with contractors and obtaining building and planning permits; many were owner-builders with little or no idea of the process involved.

The Rebuilding Advisory Service was successful in helping a lot of people through a very difficult time. Each case was different, some needed just a little advice, others required a day-by-day hands-on involvement.'

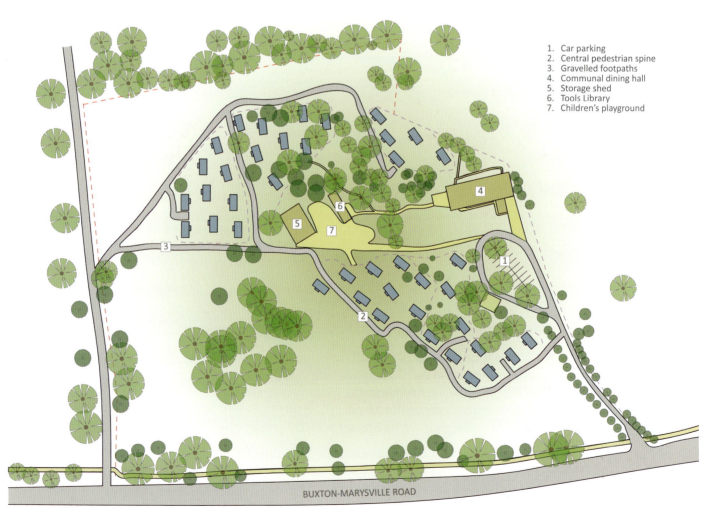

1. Car parking
2. Central pedestrian spine
3. Gravelled footpaths
4. Communal dining hall
5. Storage shed
6. Tools Library
7. Children's playground

BUXTON-MARYSVILLE ROAD

0 5 10 20M

TREES RETAINED: Site plan of the Marysville temporary village.
Source: adapted from Graham Alman.

Key project features and design aspects

Housing

The bulk of the temporary housing was comprised of 'granny flats'; ten one-bedroom and 40 two-bedroom cottages, the same designs as used in Kinglake and from the existing stock of such cottages held by the DHS Office of Housing. Some 16 single persons were accommodated in four dongas, each donga accommodating four persons in separate rooms. With a donated three-bedroom house and three acquired four-bedroom houses, altogether there were 94 dwelling units in the temporary village.

Site layout

The site plan was designed with car parking at the edges and internal circulation by paved footpaths. The cottages were placed among existing trees in a staggered pattern allowing open views from individual cottages. Community facilities were laid out around a central pedestrian spine, serving as a community hub and a public zone, leading to the more private residential areas on both sides.

INNOVATIONS: The tools library (right) and belongings storage shed (left) were important community facilities in the Marysville temporary village.

Community facilities

The main community facilities in the temporary village consisted of: a dining hall with six kitchens; a storage shed with lockers for personal belongings and valuable household items; a tools library; a community pavilion with barbeque; a children's playground; communal toilets, showers, washing machines and dryers; fenced areas for pets; and a manager's office and residence.

ROOM FOR ALL: The community dining hall in the temporary village (now used in the school camp).

Terry and Sharon build a house with a flowing curvilinear form

Terry and Sharon; their house; and the floor plan of their house.
Source: floor plan adapted from Terry and Sharon Donovan.

Terry Donovan, a former builder, and Sharon Donovan, a former schoolteacher, own and run a tourist resort in Marysville. Before the Black Saturday bushfires they lived in an old house and built four cottages on the site for their bed-and-breakfast resort. When the bushfire struck, Terry wanted to defend their property, but it became impossible because there was no water or electricity and it was too dark in the thick smoke. They took refuge in the nearby Gallipoli Park with other people as the town went up in flames.

After spending the next three months in rented accommodation, Terry and Sharon moved into the Marysville Temporary Village and stayed there for two years. 'The temporary village was a stroke of genius. It kept the community together,' says Terry. They are grateful for all the donations and support that made the village habitable. 'There was fabulous support from the whole country for the traumatised people. Even small things were taken care of – we had a toilet paper supply for a whole year!' says Sharon.

Staying at the temporary village helped Terry and Sharon to plan the rebuilding of their property, and after a year they started building a new house. Being an ex-builder, Terry had a good understanding of design, and he worked with the architect, Michael Shepherd, to design a house with a flowing curvilinear form. 'I wanted something different, but comfortable. We built the roof with metal sheet because of future fire risk, and had to cut each sheet to make the curved roof shape', says Terry. 'This house has no heating or cooling system, but is still always comfortable. In addition to its well-insulated construction, the high roof of the living room, and opening windows at night, keeps the house cool in the summer, and because it faces north it stays warm in the winter,' he explains. Sharon adds that, 'The living room is the best part of this house. It's so bright and cheerful.'

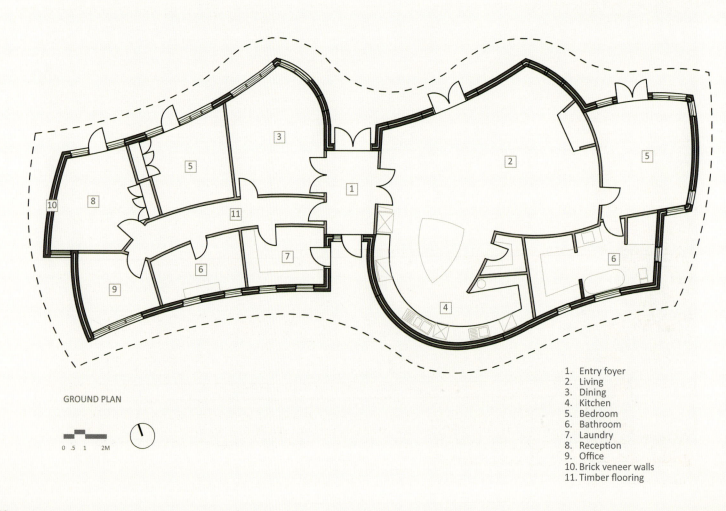

GROUND PLAN

0 .5 1   2M

1. Entry foyer
2. Living
3. Dining
4. Kitchen
5. Bedroom
6. Bathroom
7. Laundry
8. Reception
9. Office
10. Brick veneer walls
11. Timber flooring

Temporary village: 'best ever thing'

Norman Fiske, a handyman, and Rosemary Fiske, the owner of a teashop, are residents of Marysville. They have three grown-up daughters who also live in the area. Norman was driving a tourist bus in Melbourne on Black Saturday and was stuck outside the town because the roads became blocked by burnt trees. Rosemary escaped from their house just in time before it burnt down. After staying with a friend in nearby Alexandra, they sub-leased part of a house in Marysville for seven months. But then the landlord needed the house for another purpose, and Norman and Rosemary moved into the Marysville Temporary Village. Because they were among the last people who moved into the village, there was only a one-bedroom cottage available, in which they stayed for nearly two years.

In Norman's view the temporary village was designed and built 'very professionally'. 'It was the best ever thing that happened after the bushfire. It really kept our community together,' he says. Although they stayed in a small one-bedroom cottage, he has no complaints. 'All small, all tight, but quite comfortable to live in temporarily,' he says. Norman was in charge of the tools library in the village, which he continued to run even after the village changed to a school camp. 'The tools library was a great idea,' he says.

While staying at the temporary village, Norman organised his finances and he started building a new house in February 2011, completing it in six months. 'I'm glad we could stay at the temporary village and build this house,' says Norman.

Norman Fiske.

Success factors

Design sensitivity

As at Kinglake, the architectural team avoided a typical barrack-type layout and instead developed the site plan according to the site conditions and needs of the residents. Keeping the existing trees provided shade and closeness to nature; a varied and staggered layout according to the undulating terrain gave a distinctive feel to each cottage, as well as providing open views not blocked by adjacent cottages.

Although different from the layout in Kinglake, the site plan here consisted of a similar central spine with community facilities serving as a public space, and with the cottages placed away for privacy. The community facilities – storage shed, tools library, children's playground, pet-holding area – again supported the housing and provided a sense of community and belonging.

Adaptive reuse

A significant amount of resources had been invested in site development and building the temporary village. Its adaptation as a school camp after the village was closed was an effective utilisation of resources. Instead of serving only as a temporary facility, this long-term use left a positive legacy, added to the community resources of Marysville and contributed to the local economy and tourism value.

Interim solution

The temporary village provided a medium-term solution bridging emergency accommodation and permanent housing.

Community cohesion

The temporary village enabled a bushfire-affected community to remain together close to their previous place of residence and to retain their social networks, instead of undergoing disruptive relocation.

Linkage between temporary and permanent housing

The temporary village allowed residents to stay close to their destroyed homes, which helped them to undertake rebuilding. The tools library was particularly useful, providing access to a range of tools for building permanent housing.

The Rebuilding Advisory Service (RAS)

The RAS's presence in Marysville, with two roving Rebuilding Advisers, proved a valuable contribution. More than a thousand people availed themselves of advice and technical support from RAS in the bushfire-impacted areas of Victoria.[18]

The challenges

Because of the similarity in the reconstruction process in Kinglake and Marysville, a common set of reconstruction challenges became evident, as discussed below.

- Before the bushfire, the residents of the temporary village generally lived on large blocks of land and were accustomed to privacy from neighbours. Living in closer quarters with other people in the temporary village over a prolonged period was an unfamiliar experience. Despite efforts to provide a sense of community and a range of facilities, occasional friction was inevitable; anecdotal reports of public drunkenness by some residents indicate such challenges.

- The new building and planning regulations that came into place after Black Saturday also presented challenges to people who had been impacted by a major disaster and who were in an uncertain situation, particularly those who had little or no prior experience of building a house, let alone rebuilding a devastated house in a bushfire-prone area. The lack of institutional expertise, simply due to the novel nature of the new regulations, aggravated the problem. Negotiation with insurance companies, often fraught with anomalies, further compounded the situation. Thus the RAS advisers were confronted with a tremendously challenging task which, despite their significant contributions, limited their role.

Lessons learnt

Key lessons from this project include:

- The involvement of skilled architects in designing a temporary village, which is often considered unnecessary, contributed to a better understanding of the specific spatial aspirations of the residents. The value of pro bono architectural services is demonstrated by the well-designed site plans of the temporary villages. However, the example of the Re-Growth Pod in Kinglake provides a note of caution. Throughout the world architects have proposed prefabricated units as a post-disaster housing solution, but these quite often prove culturally inappropriate. The key lesson for architects is to work closely with the future occupants of their designed housing and reconstruction agencies so that their needs can be incorporated into the design.

- The importance of holding the community together through a temporary village, instead of allowing it to disintegrate through relocation was demonstrated here.

- Forming a specific institutional entity such as VBRRA that drew on the best of available governmental resources until post-disaster recovery had been achieved provides a model process.

- The RAS, although a new model, proved to be a well-utilised service. It demonstrates how skilled building professionals can play a valuable role in post-disaster reconstruction by serving as a conduit between disaster-affected communities and the technical-institutional realm of house construction.

In conclusion

The post-bushfire reconstruction process in Kinglake and Marysville followed some innovative strategies including creating a specialised agency for reconstruction, linking temporary and permanent housing, and providing technical support to affected households to rebuild their destroyed housing, and presents a model process. Communities that experienced a major upheaval were able to rebuild their new housing more resilient to future bushfires, in a context which also supported the social process of reconstructing a community after disaster.

Other notable housing reconstruction projects in Australia

Cyclone Rated Homes

Implemented in Queensland, after Cyclone Yasi (2011) and supplied and built by MiHaven. For further information, see: www.mihaven.com.au/ (accessed 1 April 2014).

Extreme Architecture

Fire- and flood-resistant houses implemented in various locations, designed by architects Ian Weir and James Davidson. For further information, see: http://eprints.qut.edu.au/57279/1/Ideas_Festival_2011_Bushfire_Ian_Weir.pdf (accessed 1 April 2014).

Grantham Reconstruction Area

Implemented in Queensland after 2011 floods by Queensland Reconstruction Authority. For further information, see: www.qldreconstruction.org.au/publications-guides/land-use-planning/rebuilding-grantham-together (accessed 1 April 2014).

Home Rebuilding Program

Implemented in Victoria after the 2009 Black Saturday bushfires by Habitat for Humanity Australia. For further information, see: www.habitat.org.au/vic (accessed 1 April 2014).

Notes

1 Parliament of Victoria, *Final Report: 2009 Victorian Bushfires Royal Commission* (Melbourne: Government Printer for the State of Victoria, 2010).
2 QUT (Queensland University of Technology) (ed.) *Impacts and Adaptation Response of Infrastructure and Communities to Heatwaves: The Southern Australian Experience of 2009* (Gold Coast, NCCARF (National Climate Change Adaptation Research Facility, 2010).
3 Parliament of Victoria, *Final Report: 2009 Victorian Bushfires Royal Commission*.
4 Ibid.
5 Standards Australia, *Construction of Buildings in Bushfire-prone Areas* (AS 3959-2009) (Sydney: Standards Australia, 2009).
6 See, for instance, Building Commission (undated) *A Guide to Building in Victoria After the Bushfires*. Available at: www.weepa.com.au/_dbase_upl/guide_building_bushfires.pdf (accessed 1 April 2014).
7 Battenbough, G. (2009) 'Nineteen firms unveil bushfire designs', *Architecture and Design* (online). Available at: www.architectureanddesign.com.au/news/industry-news/nineteen-firms-unveil-bushfire-designs (accessed 1 April 2014).
8 VBRRA (2011) *Legacy Report*. Available at: http://trove.nla.gov.au/work/159343996?selectedversion=NBD51051068 (accessed 31 March 2014).
9 Bushfire CRC (Cooperative Research Centre) (2009) 'Integrative studies', in *Victorian 2009 Bushfire Research Response: Final Report*. Available from: www.bushfirecrc.com/sites/default/files/managed/resource/chapter-5-integrated-studies.pdf (accessed 1 April 2014).
10 Parliament of Victoria, *Final Report: 2009 Victorian Bushfires Royal Commission*.
11 Victoria Police (2009) *Bushfire Death Toll Revised to 173* (media release). Available at: www.police.vic.gov.au/content.asp?Document_ID=20350 (accessed 31 March 2014).
12 VBRRA (2011) *Legacy Report*. Available at: http://trove.nla.gov.au/work/159343996?selectedversion=NBD51051068 (accessed 31 March 2014).
13 Ibid.
14 DHS (Department of Human Services) (2013) *Victorian Bushfire Appeal Fund Progress Report and Financial Information*. Available at: www.dhs.vic.gov.au/bushfireappeal/about-the-fund (accessed 1 April 2014).
15 See, for example, NSW Government, *Supporting Secondary Dwellings (Granny Flats)* (fact sheet) (Sydney: Department of Planning and Infrastructure, 2011).
16 Parliament of Victoria, *Final Report: 2009 Victorian Bushfires Royal Commission*.
17 Victoria Police, *Bushfire Death Toll Revised*.
18 Fire Recovery Unit, *Victorian Bushfire Recovery Four Year Update* (Melbourne: Department of Planning and Community Development, 2013).

Cyclone | Bangladesh

Bangladesh is under serious threat due to climate change.[1] Annual cycles of flooding, and devastating extreme weather events, are common there. The long coastline – more than 700 kilometres and home to more than 30 million people – is exposed to increasingly violent cyclones, rising sea levels, tidal flooding and salinity intrusion. Widespread poverty, the low-lying and flat topography of one of the largest riverine deltas in the world and a high population density are some of the key factors behind the country's chronic social and environmental vulnerability.

Cyclone Aila struck the coastal areas of south-western Bangladesh on 25 May 2009 with great ferocity and less than two years after the devastating 2007 Cyclone Sidr. In addition to the winds, a storm surge of more than 6 metres caused extensive havoc. Damage to coastal embankments led to widespread inundation. More than 3,000,000 people were affected, nearly 200 were killed, many more injured and displaced, and nearly 550,000 houses were destroyed or damaged.[2, 3] Outbreaks of epidemics such as diarrhoea inflicted further agony on the disaster-affected people.[4, 5, 6]

Reconstruction after disasters such as Cyclone Aila is led mainly by NGOs, with the government playing only a minor role.[7] Bangladesh remains largely rural. More than 70 per cent of the population lives in villages, despite recent rapid urbanisation,[8] and most housing reconstruction projects are rural. Urban projects are made difficult by the uncertainty of land ownership, particularly in the extensive slums of the large cities.

An ongoing question for many reconstruction agencies is whether to build durable, but more expensive, houses (for instance, with brick walls) for a smaller target group, or to build less durable, cheaper houses (for instance, with bamboo walls) for a larger group. For example, after a massive flood in 2004, a reconstruction project led by the United Nations Development Programme chose to build bamboo houses on stabilised earth plinths for more than 16,000 households;[9] building brick houses would have catered for less than a quarter of this number. Improving resilience through community-led housing reconstruction is critical. For example, UNDP in its later projects started building brick houses, which, though targeting fewer people, serve as safe refuges for the wider community.[10]

Most reconstruction projects follow the 'core house' concept – usually a single room around which extensions can be built over time – providing a sturdier version of a house typical of the local community. Even within the same community, such designs will vary according to the implementing agency.[11, 12]

The two projects that are examined in this chapter are located in the Khulna and Satkhira Districts, both which bore the brunt of Cyclone Aila. Both projects emphasise the value of a community-led approach to housing reconstruction.

◁ AT RISK: The Khulna District shoreline, typical of Bangladesh's highly vulnerable coast.

STABILISED: A UNDP-built house on an earthen plinth stabilised with cement.

Cyclone Aila, 2009

Owner-driven reconstruction

Since the 1960s, the low-lying coastal plains of the vast riverine delta of Bangladesh have been protected by government-built earthen dykes. Since their construction, they have been weakened by cyclones, human intervention and, following Cyclone Sidr in 2007, very little maintenance. When Cyclone Aila hit in 2009, the dykes collapsed, causing extensive inundation. Many communities took refuge on the parts of the dykes remaining above water, living for more than two years in makeshift shelters without basic services. Some of the most affected areas – such as Dacope Sub-district in Khulna District – were remote and, even in normal conditions, difficult to access.

Bangladesh's resource-strapped government delayed the expensive works necessary to repair the dykes, and the continuing widespread inundation impeded reconstruction. The Bangladesh Red Crescent Society (BDRCS) and other agencies provided emergency relief until the dykes were repaired and reconstruction could begin in late 2011.

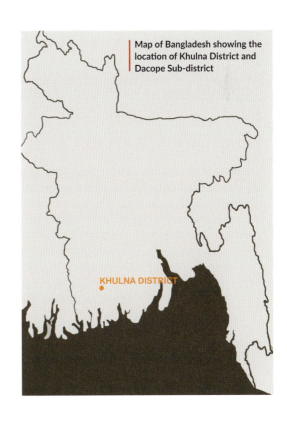

Map of Bangladesh showing the location of Khulna District and Dacope Sub-district

KHULNA DISTRICT

'The cyclone washed away the dykes and the whole area was flooded. We had to live for more than two years on a part of the dyke that survived.'

– Moyna Begum, Khulna, Bangladesh

LOW-LYING: Dacope showing and its coastal environment

Implementing agencies	
BDRCS	
Donors	
IFRC; HKRC	
	Cost
Context	**US$650 per house excluding additional**
Cyclone Aila, 2009	**investments by beneficiaries**
Location	**Type of post-disaster project**
Dacope Sub-district, Khulna district, Bangladesh	**Owner-driven housing reconstruction**
Number of houses built	**Date completed**
155 new houses	**July 2013**

Why this project case study?

In a context where most reconstruction projects are donor-driven, this BDRCS project represents a unique owner-driven example. Housing reconstruction is integrated with community infrastructure, livelihood support and disaster risk reduction. The project offers guidance on how to address the diverse needs of a vulnerable, disaster-affected community, in a remote and vulnerable location.

BDRCS built core housing after Cyclone Sidr in 2007,[13] and lessons from that project formed the basis for subsequent post-Aila projects such as this one.

Agency roles

In June 2011, the Hong Kong Red Cross (HKRC) allocated US$450,000 to the International Federation of Red Cross and Red Crescent Societies (IFRC), which then funded BDRCS to implement the project. The funding was used for emergency relief, such as food, medicine and tents, and then for reconstruction. Other funds for emergency relief had also been provided from 2009. BDRCS worked with 25 volunteers, some from the community and others who were registered BDRCS volunteers. BDRCS staff provided technical support and training on housing and community infrastructure, and local government authorities assisted in beneficiary selection.

The reconstruction process

BDRCS provided relief and other support to disaster-affected communities before reconstruction could begin in 2011. The two-year delay in repairing the dykes allowed a review of the lessons from previous projects, planning, and the identification of the neediest and most vulnerable households using IFRC's Vulnerability and Capacity Assessment Toolbox.[14] A beneficiary list was prepared in consultation with local government authorities. Extensive community consultation was undertaken to reach agreement on the owner-driven reconstruction approach and the appropriate types of community infrastructure to be provided.

Because of the area's remoteness, building materials had to be procured from cities such as Khulna and Dhaka. The owner-driven approach meant local construction workers were employed, supporting the disaster-affected local economy. Beneficiaries and construction workers were provided with training by BDRCS on 'Participatory Approach for Safe Shelter Awareness', based on the training manual developed by IFRC.

Beneficiary households were given a set of building components, as well as a sanitary latrine, a rainwater tank and a grant to purchase further building materials and to employ construction workers. Most beneficiaries contributed extra money and in many cases salvaged materials from their previous houses to build according to their needs.

Each household built a raised earthen plinth and then BDRCS's technical support staff assisted with the installation of the building components, including the latrine and rainwater tank. Finally, a grant to the household was released for completion of construction.

Adith Shah Durjoy

Senior Disaster Management Officer,
BDRCS, Dhaka

....

'I've been working at BDRCS for the last six years; I worked for GTZ and ActionAid before. I studied for an Environmental Science Masters at Khulna University and have since then worked in the field of natural resource management, which led to work in the disaster management field.

'After Cyclone Sidr in 2007 we provided contractor-built housing, which provided us with lessons leading to the adoption of an owner-driven approach in this project. We carried out consultations with cyclone-affected communities and understood that they would be able to build their own houses with some support from us.

'The project beneficiaries are happy because, together with shelter, we provided other forms of support to build their resilience.'

Mannan Ali Shaikh

Youth Volunteer,
BDRCS, Khulna

....

'I'm from Khulna and worked as a Youth Volunteer on this project. I was involved in all stages of the project.

'This area has a water problem due to salinity. That is why we prioritised improving the water supply by installing pond sand filters and rainwater tanks.

'People were expecting us to build complete houses for them, but we didn't have the budget. If we did that, we could have supported less people.

'We selected the most vulnerable people as beneficiaries. There was some interference by local powerful people who wanted their followers to benefit, but we managed to overcome that tactfully. Because we provided so much support other than housing, the whole community has benefited.'

Key project features and design aspects

Return and integration

The BDRCS project brought displaced people back to their villages after the damaged dykes were repaired, and supported recovery. An integrated reconstruction process leading to long-term community development then followed.

Housing

Each beneficiary household was provided with six reinforced concrete posts, ten pieces of corrugated iron sheet with ridge pieces, screws, washers, nails and wire for fixing them, timber and bamboo for roof framing, a sanitary latrine with walling materials for privacy, and a 1000-litre rainwater tank. Each beneficiary household was also given US$125 to buy additional materials and to pay construction workers.

Water and sanitation

Because this coastal area is affected by salinity intrusion from the sea level rise caused by climate change, groundwater is not suitable for drinking and the project promoted alternative water sources. The project repaired an existing pond sand filter to purify rainwater from a pond, and built a new pond sand filter and community rainwater tank. These facilities catered to the whole community rather than just the 155 households that received individual rainwater tanks with their housing support.

Similarly, a building for community latrines and bathrooms, consisting of six chambers (three male and three female), was built to serve the whole community. Each male and female section had a bathroom, a latrine and children's latrine.

Livelihoods

Of the 155 households that received housing support, 107 very needy households received US$125 as livelihood assistance, combined with training from local government authorities on livelihood development through fisheries, poultry and livestock keeping, and agriculture. All households in the community received fruit tree saplings to generate income. Importantly, further livelihood support was provided through a cash-for-work program for the excavation of earth and using it to elevate above flood level the playgrounds of two schools and four roads.

CLEAN: A newly built community pond sand filter.

BUILT FOR ALL: The community latrine and bathroom building.

Disaster risk reduction

The project's newly constructed roads serve as dykes, with trees planted along their edges to help prevent erosion, stabilise the slopes, and protect the dykes from collapse in future cyclones. BDRCS conducted a household awareness campaign on early warning and evacuation. The Cyclone Preparedness Program, a large BDRCS volunteer network, was extended to the area, with training and early warning equipment provided to community volunteers.

Health services

A medical team provided support for community health through promoting health awareness and education, and existing government health facilities were renovated.

Success factors

An owner-driven approach

The owner-driven approach was unusual – typically, projects in Bangladesh are donor-driven – and contributed to the project's success. With the building components and grant provided by BDRCS, and their own resources, beneficiaries could build as they preferred and control the quality of construction. BDRCS engineers and volunteers supervised to ensure further quality control, in a process that led to beneficiaries being largely satisfied with the outcome.

Good quality building components

BDRCS ensured that building components were of high quality. For example, the reinforced concrete components – posts and latrine slabs – were produced locally, but the materials – cement, sand, rods and aggregate – were procured by BDRCS in large cities, Dhaka or Khulna, where the best construction materials could be found.

Each household was given six reinforced concrete posts, instead of the four originally planned, so that the house could be sturdy. The 100mm x 100mm x 3800mm posts are strong: four reinforcement rods extend at one end to attach the wall plate and rafters; a 380mm-long T-footing at the bottom of the post is used to anchor the post into the ground; and 22 closely spaced stirrups inside the posts provide additional strength.

The corrugated iron roofing sheets are among the best available in the country. Their 0.42mm thickness helps prevent them being lifted-off in storms, compared to the 0.30mm or often much thinner sheets generally used in rural housing. The sheets are galvanised and painted to prevent rusting. All houses have a hipped roof, a design that provides better wind-resistance than a gable roof.

MULTIPLE BENEFITS: Roads built through the cash-for-work program serve as dykes.

SAFE FROM FLOODS: This school playground was raised above flood level through the cash-for-work program.

Moyna; her house; and
its floor plan.

Good-quality materials promote beneficiary satisfaction

Moyna Begum lives in Joynogor village, Dacope, with her fisherman husband and two children. Her husband was injured and made disabled in Cyclone Alia. Moyna's previous house, made of palm leaves, was washed away and her homestead was flooded for nearly three years by the storm surge. During that time she and her family lived in a plastic tent on a dyke. 'It was a time of great difficulty,' she says. They had to bathe in the salty water, which was everywhere, and there were no toilets or other services. They couldn't earn much income and depended on relief from BDRCS and other organisations.

Moyna's household received housing support from BDRCS, but no livelihood support because they were able to earn some income by fishing. With the building components and the US$125 from BDRCS, she added another US$75 from her own savings. She bought extra corrugated iron sheets, though not as good as those supplied by BDRCS, to make a front veranda. She paid a carpenter to build the house and she and household members and neighbours helped. 'It took us only five days to build the house because some of the parts were ready-made,' she says. She also bought a solar panel because there is no electricity grid in her remote area. She and her family use the nearby communal bathroom for bathing.

'We're happy with the house and the quality of the corrugated iron sheets and the reinforced concrete posts given by BDRCS, and for all their support,' she says.

GROUND FLOOR

1. Bedroom
2. Front veranda added by beneficiary
3. Earthen plinth and floor (average 1.0 m high)
4. Bamboo posts of veranda
5. Six reinforced concrete posts with T-footings
6. Corrugated iron sheet walls

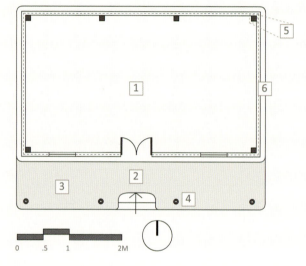

The first corrugated iron sheet roof in the area

Yusuf Ali Sikdar is a sharecropper and lives with his wife and two sons in Joynogor village, Dacope. With housing support from BDRCS and an extra US$125 from his own savings, he paid for labour to dig a fishpond and to process the earth to build his new mud-walled house. He spent funds on two extra sheets of corrugated iron to make the house larger. He also bought some cheaper corrugated iron sheets to build a front veranda. He used nylon rope to tie the roof of his house to the ground. 'I'm scared of another storm, so I'm trying to keep my new house safe,' he said. He was happy for the support he received: 'BDRCS saved us; without them we wouldn't have survived. We've never had a house with a corrugated iron roof in this area and now I own one!'

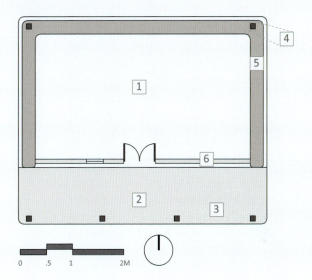

Yusuf; his house; and its floor plan.

GROUND FLOOR
1. Bedroom
2. Front veranda added by beneficiary
3. Earthen plinth and floor (average 1.0 m high)
4. Six reinforced concrete posts with T-footings
5. Mud walls
6. Rough timber wall

Comprehensive community infrastructure

Infrastructure support was provided at both the household level and the community level. At the household level, the rainwater tank and latrine provided vital infrastructure. At the community level, pond sand filters, a rainwater tank and the communal toilet/bathroom provided vital infrastructure. This two-pronged approach allowed the most vulnerable households to be targeted, while also meeting wider community needs. Housing beneficiaries also used the community facilities, especially the bathroom, because most of their houses did not have any bathing provision.

Attention to detail helped. For example, solar-powered lights in the community toilet provide safety for women at night; small toilet pans in the children's latrine make it easier for them to use. And BDRCS ensured good quality construction and materials.

An integrated approach

Integration of housing with community infrastructure and welfare components was important in this remote area where such facilities were negligible. Project support for improvement of health services was crucial.

Effective disaster risk reduction

By taking BDRCS's Cyclone Preparedness Program to the region, training local volunteers and raising community awareness, the project helped to overcome the region's remoteness and provided for the first time a local early warning system, significantly improving the community's disaster preparedness. Roads that, through being built, provided income to the community, also double as flood-protection dykes. House plinths raised a metre above ground level protect houses from flooding.

Livelihood support

It was essential to revive livelihoods in this impoverished area. The most needy and vulnerable households received support, and a cash-for-work program also brought income and at the same time raised playgrounds and roads above flood level and benefited the wider community.

Extensive experience

The Red Cross movement has long-standing humanitarian experience, and its large global network and access to resources allowed this project to be implemented in a highly effective manner. BDRCS is well-known and respected in the area, which meant communities and local authorities welcomed its presence and extended their cooperation.

The challenges

Significant challenges included:

- The long-term sustainability of the project is threatened by the flat low-lying coastal areas of Bangladesh being exposed to climate change impacts, particularly sea level rise.
- Poor infrastructure and transportation cause isolation, and emigration was common, with further implications for the project's long-term value.
- Security was a key challenge. For example, beneficiaries feared theft of the rainwater tanks outside their houses. Some beneficiaries lifted their tanks onto the veranda or moved them closer to the house for safety. Surveillance was necessary, adding to the beneficiaries' workload.

Lessons learnt

Key lessons from this project include:

- The owner-driven approach offered advantages over donor-driven housing projects, especially by creating better beneficiary satisfaction. The approach was more effective when backed by quality assurance and supervision by the implementing agency.
- Integrating housing and infrastructure, instead of only building houses, will help create resilient communities.
- Targeting the neediest households with housing support, while at the same time providing infrastructure that benefits the whole community, is an effective way to use a limited budget.
- The good design quality of the housing provided, and the infrastructure that benefits the whole community, have made the beneficiaries and their community more resilient to future disasters.
- When good quality materials are not available locally, the strategy of procuring materials from reliable sources and transporting them to the project area, when backed by supervision and quality control, proves an effective approach to working in remote and isolated locations.

In conclusion

Even in difficult post-disaster circumstances in a remote location, success can be achieved in reconstruction projects as demonstrated in this case study. The BDRCS project was notable for its owner-driven housing, rare in the reconstruction field in Bangladesh, and even globally. The key achievement of this approach was greater beneficiary satisfaction, because affected communities were able to build their houses according to individual needs. The integration of housing with community infrastructure was also very important in this remote location with scanty infrastructure and services.

AQUACULTURE: A view from Shyamnagar showing its low-lying environment and large fish-farming ponds.

Cyclone Aila, 2009
Community-based reconstruction

Satkhira is an outlying district in the south-western corner of Bangladesh. Transport links are poor, with widespread and large aquaculture ponds making it difficult to plan adequate transportation infrastructure. The storm surge that came with Cyclone Aila in 2009 inundated the area, marooning communities and severing even the tenuous connections that had existed. Part of the post-disaster recovery process involved re-establishing these connections, a necessary precondition for housing reconstruction. Nevertheless, boat transport remains predominant, and most project building materials had to be brought in by boat.

The beneficiary community of 300 people, who were settled on a linear strip of land surrounded by water in the mid-1980s under a government program, had their entire community swept away. The project re-established the settlement and reconstructed housing.

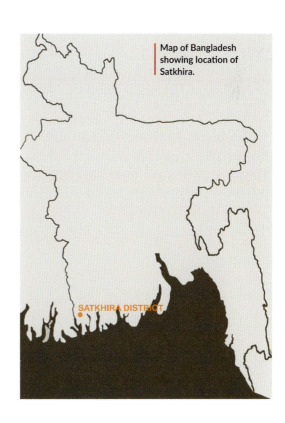

Map of Bangladesh showing location of Satkhira.

SATKHIRA DISTRICT

'The wave that came with the cyclone washed away all the three houses of my family. I held onto a broken tree and floated to the next village.'

– Saleha Khatun, Satkhira, Bangladesh

WATER FOR MANY NEEDS: Ponds in front of each house provide fish and are used for bathing and washing.

Implementing agencies
Department of Architecture, BRAC University
Key partners: Shushilan; Dream Bangla; Rupantar;
Water Development Board of Bangladesh; UNDP;
BRAC

Donors
UNDP; BRAC

Context
Cyclone Aila, 2009

Location
Shyamnagar Sub-district, Satkhira District,
Bangladesh

Number of houses built
43 new houses

Cost
US$1500 per house
Total project cost = US$125,000

Type of post-disaster project
Reconstruction of housing

Date completed
November 2011

Why this project case study?

The project was developed by academics from the School of Architecture, BRAC University, Dhaka, and enabled student participation to promote real-world learning. The project offers lessons on how built environment professionals and students can facilitate community participation processes to build effective post-disaster housing.

This project was led by two very prominent agencies – the Bangladesh Rural Advancement Committee (BRAC), one of the largest NGOs in the world, and the United Nations Development Programme (UNDP), one of the largest agencies in the United Nations system.

The project also highlights the vulnerability of coastal communities in Bangladesh that live under the continual threat of climate change and related disasters. It also underlines the strong need to address this vulnerability, and demonstrates that even under difficult circumstances effective and community-led housing reconstruction is possible.

Agency roles

UNDP provided the bulk of the project funding, approximately US$125,000. BRAC donated half of the US$4400 to build a primary school. UNDP provided funds to several NGOs to implement parts of the project. BRAC University's Department of Architecture was responsible for building design and the supervision of construction.

Dykes damaged by the cyclone were repaired by the government's Water Development Board. Homestead land and roads were raised above flood level by a prominent local NGO, Shushilan, which also planted trees along roads to prevent erosion, and provided trees for planting on homesteads to stabilise land and produce fruits. Shushilan helped excavate fishponds in front of each house that serve as a source of food and income (fish, ducks) and for bathing and washing. Another NGO, Rupantar, provided grants, livestock and poultry for livelihoods. The NGO Dream Bangla provided rainwater tanks and sanitary latrines.

Khondaker Hasibul Kabir

Architect/Senior Lecturer,
BRAC University, Dhaka

'I studied architecture at the Bangladesh University of Engineering and Technology and did a Master's in Landscape Architecture at Sheffield University, UK. After I graduated, I worked on several participatory action research projects on developing flood-resistant housing and my interest in this field grew from that.

This area doesn't have a nearby cyclone shelter so we decided to design the houses as mini cyclone shelters. Each house can be a safe refuge during a cyclone without any need for evacuation.

This is a cohesive community and it was good to work with the people to build their resilience. We gave a lot of effort to community consultations. The community ran the project; this was their project.'

Henri Markus Stalder

Disaster Recovery Specialist,
UNDP, Dhaka

'I was trained as a construction entrepreneur, a field with several cross-cutting segments including project and business management in the construction sector. I have worked widely in Asia after the 2004 Indian Ocean tsunami in Indonesia, Thailand and Sri Lanka.

I joined UNDP in February 2012 after the project was completed. I've used my experience of this project and the lessons learnt from it in other housing projects. We are building another 265 houses in Koyra, near the project area, also designed to be resilient.

In this project, sanitation and waste management are important issues that have not yet been fully addressed. We are planning a second stage where we will deal with these issues. We have the funds now to replace the wooden walls with brick and repair the tile roofs where they leak.'

The reconstruction process

Before reconstruction could begin, it was necessary for the government's Water Development Board to repair the damaged dykes and drain the inundation. Washed away and eroded roads and settlements were then repaired and raised above water level.

Community consultations, undertaken by BRAC University's design team, played a significant role in the project. The design team included an architect, architecture students and an engineer originally from Satkhira District with good local knowledge. A community animator from Simple Action for the Environment – a rural-based organisation in northern Bangladesh – co-facilitated the community consultations.

Styrofoam shrimp packing boxes, freely available in this area of widespread aquaculture, and other local materials were used to make models, and for a month the community worked to model 'dream houses'. The models all indicated a desire for two-storey houses, reflecting the trauma each participant had experienced.

After the model making, 15 local construction workers and three women representatives were invited to BRAC University in Dhaka to participate in a workshop with the design team, students and engineers from the government's Housing and Building Research Institute. The workshop reinforced the community's preference for two-storey houses.

Construction followed. The houses and primary school were built for free, mostly by local construction workers and people from the community, which saved funds and gave the community a sense of ownership. The reinforced concrete work, however required skilled workers from beyond the community. Technical supervision was provided by the design team, with some members spending extended periods in the area.

HIGH AND DRY: By piling earth from pond excavations, the settlement is raised to protect it from high water.

MODEL APPROACH: The design workshop with community members at BRAC University. Source: Khondaker Hasibul Kabir.

Cyclone-affected people need houses foremost

Saleha Khatun lives with eight others in the first house built in the BRAC–UNDP project in Shyamnagar. She is a housewife and her husband is a daily labourer. Her three sons, two of them married with children, are part of the extended family. Because of the lack of space in her one-room house, her sons built another house, with corrugated iron sheet walls and thatched roof, on her land. Her married daughter lives next door in a house also built through the project. Saleha extended the undercroft of her house on all four sides with thatched awnings on bamboo framing, making the ground level a larger and more shaded space.

Saleha's previous bamboo and thatch house had been washed away by the storm surge that came with Cyclone Aila. She survived by clinging to a piece of debris that carried her to safety. She and her family stayed in a makeshift tent on a dyke for nearly two years until this house was completed. She says that when people from BRAC came and asked the disaster-affected people of the community what they needed most, 'All the people told them that we have nothing left now, but we first need a house because we have become homeless.'

Saleha; her house; and its floor plan. Source: floor plan adapted from: Khondaker Hasibul Kabir.

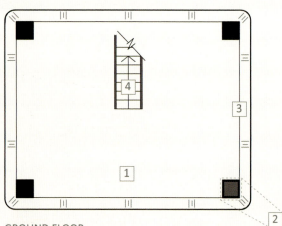

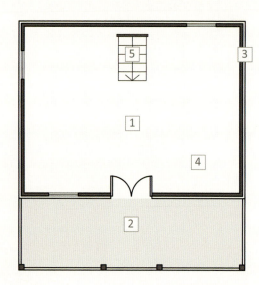

GROUND FLOOR
1. Flexible, multipurpose undercroft space
2. Four reinforced concrete columns as part of reinforced concrete frame
3. Compacted earthen floor and plinth 300–500 mm above ground level
4. Wooden ladder enclosed for extra indoor space or extended

0   .5   1   2M

FIRST FLOOR
1. Bedroom
2. Balcony
3. Timber walls
4. Timber floor
5. Trapdoor

A hard-working, honest organisation

Anisur Rahman lives in Shyamnagar in a house built in the BRAC-UNDP reconstruction project. Before the cyclone he was a shrimp farmer, but his ponds were destroyed and later bought by a wealthier farmer. He became unemployed and makes a living from odd jobs.

He, his wife, three daughters and son live in an extended family of eighteen people with his two brothers and their families. One of his brothers also received a house, located on a homestead immediately adjacent to Anisur's house. Because the third brother also wanted a house, all three brothers invested extra money to join the two houses into one large house. They also built a large veranda with corrugated iron sheet roofing and reinforced concrete posts. Because the timber walls were getting spoilt in the saline and humid environment, the family has painted the house with bituminous tar; and where gaps had appeared, they fixed metal strips to stop rain penetration. 'These strips have begun rusting, I'll have to also paint them with tar,' Anisur notes.

Anisur is a community leader and played an important role in the consultations with the design team. He was one of the fifteen workers who attended the design workshop in Dhaka at BRAC University and, with two other community members, led negotiations with the design team. He says of the design team, 'They worked very hard and honestly. This was the most honest organisation that's ever worked in this area. I will remember them till I die.' He was also pleased with the two-storey stilt house design. 'It has a great advantage. An extra room can be added below. The children also love it – they can play running up and down,' he said.

Anisur; and his house.

Key features of the project

Housing

Each house was built on a raised homestead above water level, a plinth of earth further raised by about a metre. Houses were elevated 3 metres above the plinth level on four reinforced concrete columns joined below the ground by reinforced concrete grade beams and at the top by reinforced concrete tie beams, thus forming a frame. On one side the tie beams were cantilevered to support a balcony. The main house structure has a single room with a balcony on one side, timber flooring and walls, and clay tile roofing on a timber frame. A wooden ladder provides access from ground level. Of 43 households, only one chose to build with a palm leaf thatch roof.

The site plan

The linear settlement consists of a set of contiguous homesteads. Each homestead has a fishpond in front, and the soil from excavating the pond was used to raise the homestead land. The fishpond boundaries serve as walkways to access the houses from a small unpaved road that runs in front of the homesteads and that connects to the mainland. There are large water bodies in front and behind the settlement, and most transport is by boat. There are no motorised vehicles on the settlement.

A primary school

The primary school built through the project is elevated above ground in a manner similar to the houses of the settlement. It has a reinforced concrete floor and brick walls, unlike the housing's timber floors and walls, and the brick walls are perforated for ventilation in the hot-humid climate. There are two classrooms with a corridor between, and a playground.

Water and sanitation

Sanitary latrines and rainwater tanks were provided. Some households sank hand-pumps for extra water. There is no electricity supply. Solar panels are available through NGO microcredit programs, and some households have installed them.

Livelihood support

UNDP channelled livelihood support through the NGO Rupantar, and each household was given US$125, two sheep, 16 ducklings and four chickens. Unfortunately, and despite good intentions, cold weather in this exposed location, and lack of experience in rearing livestock and poultry, led to the deaths of some households' animals.

Success factors

Disaster-resilient housing

In Bangladesh, before a cyclone, at-risk communities are encouraged to evacuate to cyclone shelters because their housing is generally not sturdy enough to be safe. Because there are no nearby cyclone shelters in the project area, each house was built to be a 'mini cyclone shelter'. The raised houses, with their robust reinforced concrete frames, keep people safe from winds and storm surges. The reinforced concrete work is of high quality and uses stone aggregate that provides better performance in the saline environment compared to the typical brick chips widely used in Bangladesh. After casting, the concrete was sealed to prevent loss of water and consequent cracking. And the steel reinforcements were given extra depth of cover to prevent rusting. Cross-bracings in the walls, metal straps securing the roof frame, and closer spacing of purlins near the roof eaves improve wind-resistance. Each roof tile is screwed onto the timber frame to avoid displacement by wind.

Climate-sensitive design

Houses are designed for the hot-humid climate. Being raised on columns allows them to receive cooling breezes, and balconies face the prevailing southerly winds. The project improves on typical thermal comfort by reviving a local tradition of using clay tiles for roofing, rather than the corrugated iron sheets predominant as roofing in rural areas. Timber walls provide additional thermal performance.

Flexibility of space

House undercrofts can be enclosed to create extra indoor space for large households. In most cases, when this option was taken up, because most people could not afford them, the lower floor was not built of materials that would remain undamaged in a cyclone. However, the sturdy upper floor still allows inhabitants a safe refuge.

A community-based approach

Extensive community consultations tailored the housing to community needs. Innovative activities such as model-making and a design workshop were genuine aids to community participation. Using construction skills from within the community not only saved money, which could then be invested into further housing, but also led to a sense of ownership.

University involvement brought access to a wider range of resources than otherwise would have been possible. UNDP paid for the design work undertaken by the architecture department, providing an incentive for BRAC University's support. Student volunteers contributed to the project's cost-effectiveness while and at the same time gaining valuable experience for future work in this field.

PRIMARY: The school is a key community facility.

Community facilities and services

Building a primary school addressed an essential community need. Latrines and rainwater provided basic necessities. Fishponds not only serve as a source of food and income, and a facility for bathing and washing, but also, through their excavation, provided a supply of earth to raise the homesteads.

Livelihoods

The livelihood grant gave much-needed cash to an impoverished disaster-affected community, helping beneficiaries pay for essentials, such as the medical services for which the community had to struggle to obtain even in normal times. Although the provision of livestock and poultry was not entirely successful, in the cases where the animals did survive, they provided both a source of income and subsistence.

Project challenges

Despite positive intentions and strong efforts, many unanticipated challenges arose after project completion:

- Housing was built prior to community facilities, which in retrospect, was a mistake. By building community facilities first, greater rapport with the community might have been developed, which might then have led to a better community contribution to the housing component of the project. The school was built late, when the community was exhausted after building the housing, and so community members were not able to provide full support. Beginning with the housing component created a sense of dependency and individualism, which then made the community less willing to contribute to building the facilities that would benefit the whole community.

- Through the design process, the community and the design team reached agreement on building timber walls and using clay tile roofing. These materials are, however, uncommon, and it became difficult to ensure the quality of the products and workmanship. The timber walls suffered in the humid and saline environment and, due to poor construction, rain penetrated through gaps between the timber siding and roofing tiles. The timber walls had to be replaced eventually with brick and the roofs repaired to prevent leaks.

- Despite the efforts of various agencies, basic services and infrastructure remain inadequate, perhaps a reflection of the broader national context. Inadequate awareness and unfamiliarity with, and lack of training in the use of such products as sanitary latrines and rainwater tanks mean they are not being used to best advantage. Open defecation is still practised by some, and people are drinking contaminated water from surrounding water bodies, leading to gastro-intestinal diseases.

- The settlement is in a precarious location, being surrounded by water, and the entire Bangladeshi coast is exposed to climate change impacts, including sea level rise, making the long-term sustainability of the project a key challenge.

Lessons learnt

This was a unique project in terms of its setting and the way it was implemented, and offered a series of lessons:

- Of particularly note is the extensive and innovative community consultation process, which has potential for wider adoption.

- An approach situated between owner-driven and donor-driven strategies was fruitful, with donor and community priorities mediated by a design team.

- Engaging with the community should not necessarily end after project completion. In this project, where a second stage is being implemented, reconstruction can become a bridge to long-term development and longer-term commitment by agencies.

- In such a precarious and vulnerable location, reducing the risk of future disaster impacts has been rightly prioritised, supporting the imperative of building resilient housing

In conclusion

This Satkhira housing reconstruction project is an example of a good outcome within the constraints of a highly difficult geographic and economic situation. The project demonstrates that architects can effectively contribute to post-disaster housing reconstruction, combining design processes, such as using scale models, with innovative participatory development methods. The case study also shows large and prominent development agencies such as BRAC and UNDP supporting small-scale rural projects. Finally, the project points to the necessity of addressing the extreme vulnerability of coastal communities in Bangladesh, through specific community design and technical interventions.

Other notable housing reconstruction projects in Bangladesh

Bangladesh has a highly active NGO sector with many agencies working in the reconstruction field, and the selection of projects below is only a small sample. Because post-Aila reconstruction work only began in 2011, project documentation is scarce. For further information on some of the key agencies that implemented post-Aila housing projects, see:

Riquet, D. (2012) *Review of Development Partners' Response to Cyclone Aila.* Dhaka: Ministry of Disaster Management and Relief.

Core shelter

Implemented in Pirojpur, Patuakhali, Barguna and Bagerhat districts, after Cyclone Sidr (2007) by the International Federation of Red Cross and Red Crescent Societies (IFRC). For further information, see:

www.ifrc.org/docs/appeals/07/mdrbd003fr.pdf (accessed: 6 February 2014) and www.disasterassessment.org/documents/B.3%20Bangladesh%20-%202007%20-%20Cyclone%20Sidr.pdf (accessed 6 February 2014).

Disaster resilient habitat

Implemented in Dacope, Khulna, after Cyclone Aila (2009) by the Comprehensive Disaster Management Programme (CDMP), Ministry of Disaster Management & Relief, Government of Bangladesh. For further information, see:

www.preventionweb.net/files/30537_30537bangladeshdisasterclimateresil.pdf (accessed 6 February 2014).

Family shelter (with rainwater harvesting)

Implemented in Bagerhat after Cyclone Sidr (2007) by CARE. For further information, see:

www.carebangladesh.org/publication/Publication_8577968.pdf (accessed 6 February 2014).

Flood-resistant shelter and sanitation

Implemented in Debhata, Satkhira, after Cyclone Aila (2009) by Islamic Relief. For further information, see:

www.irwbd.org/programlist/fresswrbd (accessed 6 February 2014).

Post-flood family shelter

Implemented in 23 flood-affected districts in Bangladesh after flood (2004) by United Nations Development Programme (UNDP) and eight partner NGOs. For further information, see:

UNDP (2004) Fix the Risk (video documentary), Dhaka, UNDP (United Nations Development Programme).

Notes

1 Dasgupta, S. *et al.*, 'The impact of sea level rise on developing countries: a comparative analysis', World Bank Policy Research Working Paper No. 4136. (Washington, DC: World Bank, 2007).

2 BDRCS, *Early Recovery Response for Cyclone Aila Affected Most Vulnerable People of Khulna District, Bangladesh* (project proposal) (Dhaka: BDRCS (Bangladesh Red Cross and Red Crescent Societies), 2011).

3 Hong Kong Red Cross (2009) *Bangladesh Cyclone Aila: Work Report 1*. Available at: www.redcross.org.hk/en/disasterrelief_prepard/international_projects/ipappeal_update_detail.html?year=2009&id=409 (accessed 10 October 2013).

4 FPP (Forest Peoples Programme) (2009) 'Cyclone Aila's devastation of the Bangladesh coast: another victim of climate change?'. Available at: www.forestpeoples.org/region/bangladesh/news/2010/10/cyclone-aila-s-devastation-bangladesh-coast-another-victim-climate-ch (accessed 25 October 2013).

5 IFRC, *Bangladesh: Cyclone Aila.* Final Report (Geneva: IFRC (International Federation of Red Cross and Red Crescent Societies), 2010).

6 Tran, M., 'Bangladesh villagers still struggling after Cyclone Aila's devastation', *The Guardian*, 6 March 2012.

7 Siddik, M.A. *et al. Cyclone Sidr and the Housing Sector* (Saarbrucken: Lambert Academic Publishing, 2012).

8 World Bank (2012) 'World Bank Indicators: Bangladesh – Rural Population'. Available at: www.tradingeconomics.com/bangladesh/rural-population-percent-of-total-population-wb-data.html (accessed 11 November 2013).

9 UNDP, *Fix the Risk* (documentary video). (Dhaka, UNDP (United Nations Development Programme), 2005).

10 Flinn, B. and Beresford, P., *Post-Sidr Family Shelter Reconstruction Bangladesh* (London: Department for International Development (DFID), 2009).

11 Kabir, R., *Post Cyclone Sidr Family Shelter Construction in Bangladesh: Documentation of Plans and Processes* (Dhaka: UNDP (United Nations Development Programme), 2009).

12 Seraj, S.M. and Ahmed, I., *Building Safer Houses in Rural Bangladesh* (Dhaka: Bangladesh University of Engineering and Technology (BUET), 2004).

13 UNHCR, IFRC and UN-Habitat, *Shelter Projects 2009* (Geneva: UNHCR (United Nations Human Rights Commission), IFRC (International Federation of Red Cross and Red Crescent Societies) and UN-Habitat, 2010).

14 IFRC, *VCA Toolbox* (Geneva: IFRC (International Federation of Red Cross and Red Crescent Societies), 2007).

Earthquake |
Haiti

The seismically active island of Haiti has a long history of natural disasters. On 12 January 2010, a 7.0-magnitude earthquake struck with terrible force, killing 220,000 people and injuring more than 300,000. Almost 200,000 houses were badly damaged and more than 100,000 were destroyed, suddenly 1.5 million Haitian citizens were homeless. [1, 2]

Haiti is one of the poorest countries in the world.[3] Before the 2010 earthquake, 55 per cent of the population lived on less than US$1.25 per day. Hurricane Hanna had struck in 2008, affecting 800,000 people. In the capital city, Port-au-Prince, 90 per cent of all buildings were built informally and 86 per cent of the population were living in slums in tightly-packed, poorly-built buildings.[4] The scale of the devastation from the 2010 earthquake was a direct consequence of this extreme vulnerability.

After the earthquake, community infrastructure and services were at best minimal in both urban and rural areas of the country. It was imperative to use physical reconstruction as a process of integrating housing and community infrastructure and as a means of addressing a wide range of social and economic issues, beyond only building houses.

The challenges to housing reconstruction were legion in such a context. For example, the huge quantity of debris from collapsed buildings impeded reconstruction, and its removal was costly and cumbersome.[5] Widespread informal land ownership also exacerbated the situation, making it difficult to provide new housing through a clear institutional process.

Most humanitarian agencies working in Haiti decided to build lightweight timber transitional shelters. There are many obstacles to building permanent housing, and temporary shelters were relatively quick to build and provided people living in temporary camps with some security from further earthquakes, cyclones, rain and flooding. The subsequent building of 115,000 lightweight timber transitional shelters led to other problems, using up to a third of the reconstruction budget,[6] and creating extensive transitional camps that proliferated and consolidated public health hazards. And, as a consequence, despite the vast need for permanent housing, only approximately 5,000 new houses had been built by humanitarian agencies two and a half years after the earthquake.[7]

In Port-au-Prince, projects such as the 400-house development in Zoranje, funded by the Inter-American Development Bank, relocated people to new settlements built on open land.[8] Although such projects could start from scratch and avoid the problems that plagued informally developed areas, they had other problems, such as the lack of local employment opportunities and community infrastructure and services.

In rural areas, permanent housing could be built more easily than in urban areas. For example in rural south-eastern Haiti, 500 earthquake-and cyclone-resistant houses were built by CRAterre (with funding from Misereor) within two years of the earthquake.[9, 10]

Housing reconstruction in Haiti after the 2010 earthquake required addressing a range of social, economic and other issues, beyond the building of houses. The following case studies illustrate such an approach and show that in-situ reconstruction enables communities to maintain their existing social networks and livelihood opportunities in a way that relocation or 'greenfield' housing projects may not.

◁ VULNERABLE: Informal settlements such as this are widespread in Port-au-Prince, Haiti.

A newly built settlement at Zoranje, north of Port-au-Prince.

Earthquake, 2010

Community redevelopment program

Villa Rosa had grown informally over 30 years, and prior to the 2010 earthquake had become a large informal settlement of 10,500 people. Located at the southern edge of Port-au-Prince, it was densely built, with plots of land as small as 10 square metres, and buildings up to four storeys precariously built on hillsides without any site stabilisation such as retaining walls, levelling or compacting. Movement inside the settlement was through a network of narrow pedestrian walkways, with very limited vehicular access.[11]

Typically, the buildings were made of concrete block masonry confined within a reinforced concrete frame, and used poor-quality materials. Community infrastructure and services were generally lacking. Poor drainage, poor sanitation and inferior waste management posed serious public health hazards.

When the earthquake hit in 2010, 60 per cent of the Villa Rosa settlement was devastated. Out of 1,335 houses, 595 were completely destroyed and 260 were damaged. The high density and lack of access made search-and-rescue almost impossible.

Map of Haiti showing the location of Port-au-Prince.

PORT-AU-PRINCE

'The earthquake has destroyed my life;
I survived only by God's grace.'

– Mutilus Claudette, Villa Rosa, Haiti

POOR-QUALITY: A view of Villa Rosa.

Implementing agencies
Cordaid; Build Change; AFH
Key partners: IOM; CHF; Casek (local authority)

Donors
Cordaid (main), Trocaire and UN-Habitat

Context
Earthquake, 2010

Location
Villa Rosa, Port-au-Prince, Haiti

Number of houses built
171 new houses
346 retrofitted houses

Cost
US$3500 per new house
US$1500 per retrofit; average house size 19
square metres
Costs reflect amount granted. Additional monies
supplied by homeowners

Type of post-disaster project
Owner-driven reconstruction and retrofitting
with integrated community infrastructure

Date completed
End of 2012

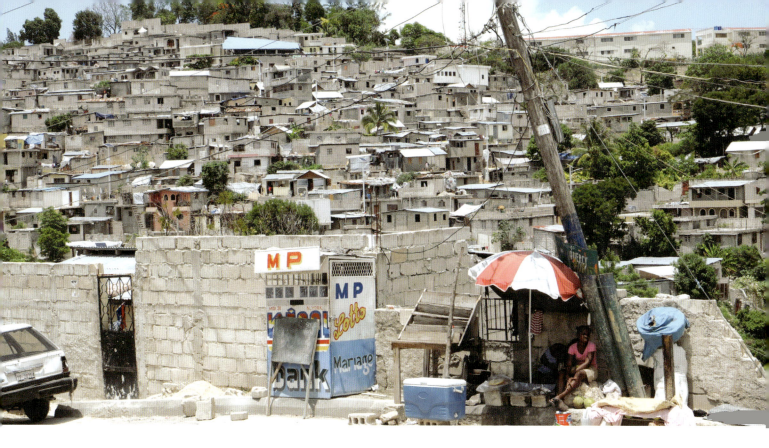

Why this project case study?

The Villa Rosa project used post-disaster reconstruction as an opportunity to develop and implement a community-based redevelopment and housing plan. It offers useful lessons on how such housing reconstruction can be undertaken in situ in a densely built, urban, poor, informal settlement, working with the disaster-affected community.

A key reason for selecting this case study is its community-based owner-driven reconstruction process, supported by the development of local skills and capacity, particularly in hazard-resistant construction. The project is also notable for its integration of housing with community infrastructure, and its implementation through partnership between agencies.

Agency roles

Cordaid led the Villa Rosa project, providing funding, coordinating agency stakeholders and selecting beneficiaries, as well as supporting the community through the process, building the capacity of the community leaders and community-based organisations. Housing reconstruction and repair were the responsibility of Build Change, a USA-based organisation specialising in earthquake-resistant construction. Build Change also provided training to local builders, raised homeowner awareness of earthquake-resistant construction, developed house designs through beneficiary consultations, and provided supervision and construction management support. Architecture for Humanity (AFH) undertook the physical planning and construction of community infrastructure, including community action planning, and the production of a rebuilding manual and an inventory of housing typologies.

Other agencies also played a role: the International Organisation for Migration (IOM) provided water, sanitation and health components. Global Communities (formerly CHF International) ran a cash-for-work program for debris removal. Because the area had been an informal settlement, it was necessary to regularise tenure security to enable reconstruction, and the local authority, Casek, supported this process by giving land titles to house owners.

This project represents the first stage of a long-term community action plan developed by AFH with the support of UN-Habitat and Cordaid to provide guidance on physical and economic planning for Villa Rosa.[12]

The reconstruction process

The housing reconstruction process was led by Build Change. In consultation with beneficiaries, Build Change architects and engineers developed the designs for housing and retrofitting. Once designs were completed, the first 60 per cent funding tranche was given to the beneficiaries, who then appointed local builders trained by Build Change.

Construction was supervised by Build Change staff, with a further funding tranche of 35 per cent provided to the beneficiaries upon satisfactory progress, and the final 5 per cent tranche given upon completion. For new houses, the US$3500 provided was usually not enough to complete construction, and beneficiaries were expected to contribute their own funds to complete their houses. Generally the final works that beneficiaries paid for were plastering and painting.

Two-storey houses were built on some of the smallest plots. All new and retrofitted single storey houses included provision for building an extra storey in the future.

Anna Wachtmeister

Architect and Urban Programme Officer, Cordaid

'This project had a multi-actor set-up – while Cordaid provided €20,000,000 for four such neighbourhoods, including Villa Rosa, we also coordinated the range of actors. Because of this, we could follow an integrated approach, incorporating infrastructure into the housing reconstruction program.

The houses built are improved versions of Haitian houses. As this was an in-situ reconstruction program, we had to work on very small sites, so all the houses have provision for vertical extension.

We were also responsible for beneficiary selection with the local authority Casek, and we selected the most affected and vulnerable households.'

Noll Tufani

Director of Programs, Build Change

'Build Change is a multifaceted agency focusing on earthquake-resistant housing. Our approach is to help build permanent housing together with strong local capacity building.

In the reconstruction process here in Haiti, we have trained hundreds of local builders and construction workers, as well as homeowners. We expect the capacity to build disaster-resilient buildings to remain with the community.

Now we are reaching out through the government to train engineers in Haiti and to raise awareness about ways to build safer houses.'

Nancy Doran

Director of Planning Studio, AFH

'I'm trained as an architect and have been recently working in urban design and planning.

We followed a bottom-up participatory planning process in Villa Rosa and developed the community infrastructure through community 'charettes'. The community's validation is important in such projects.

We got US$20,000 from the Nike Foundation to build a basketball court – a main recreational area in the community.

We have worked with UN-Habitat to develop a community action plan, which will guide the long-term development of the area.'

Key project features and design aspects

Resilient housing

All retrofitted and new houses were built using earthquake- and hurricane-resistant construction techniques. Building elements – foundations, walls and roofs – were strengthened with steel reinforcements, bracings and straps. The structural frame (columns and beams) was reinforced. A ring beam was added, an element largely missing in previous houses, its absence a key reason for many building collapses. Good-quality corrugated iron sheet was used for the roof cladding. Reconstruction was combined with extensive local capacity building and awareness-raising activities.

Community infrastructure

Through a community action plan, the community prioritised the specific upgrading of infrastructure that was considered important. Built community infrastructure included paved walkways, underground drainage, solar-powered streetlights, landscaping of public areas and a basketball court that was very popular with the community's youth.

Water, sanitation and health

A wide range of water, sanitation and health services were provided, including community and household latrines, repair of hand-pumps, drilling of wells, and improvements in solid waste management.

Cash-for-work

The cash-for-work program to remove debris allowed community members to earn desperately needed cash while at the same time creating the circumstances in which reconstruction could begin.

INFRASTRUCTURE: Walkways, drainage and streetlights built by AFH.

Beneficiary pleased with project despite an overcrowded situation

Tesie Lems now lives with his wife, child, sister and two brothers in a small two-room single-storey house built through this project. He also benefited from the CHF cash-for-work debris removal program. His previous house had collapsed; he was provided a temporary shelter and the house he now lives in was completed in November 2012.

The house was built in an owner-driven process by a Build Change-trained builder with a five-member construction team. Tesie and his household members also helped – carrying materials, fetching water, etc.

There was provision for adding an upper floor, but Tesie didn't have money for that, which is why they live in such an overcrowded arrangement. Although a small latrine has been provided, a kitchen couldn't be built on such a small plot, so the household cooks and eats outside in the narrow space between the house and its neighbour. Despite such limitations, Tesie is happy to have received the house. 'It's a good project,' he says.

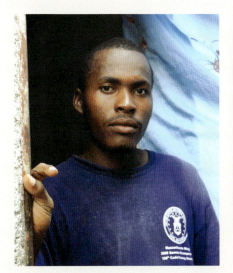

Tesie; and his house.

Rental income for a disabled person

Clerge Gerald lives alone in a small two-storey house next to the basketball court. He was badly injured in the earthquake, lost his right leg and now uses an artificial limb. He still manages to work as a security guard at the Ministry of Youth, Sports and Civic Action, though his salary is very small.

When asked why he was given a two-story house when he lived alone, he replies that it was given so that he could earn rental income: 'They were kind; seeing my condition they knew that I really needed a secure source of income.'

– 22 May 2013

Clerge. His house is the red one beside the basketball court.

Mutilus; her house; and its floor plan.
Source: adapted floor plan from Noll Tufani.

1. Bedroom
2. Dining room converted to closet
3. Reinforced concrete frame
4. Confined masonry concrete block walls
5. Reinforced concrete floor

FIRST FLOOR

0   .5   1   2M

A beneficiary lacking sufficient funds lives in an unfinished house

Mutilus Claudette now lives in a single-room dwelling on the first floor of a two-storey building built through the project. She received this house because her previous house was completely destroyed. Her husband died before the earthquake; she lives here with her two sons, one 12 years old and the other 21. All three of them sleep on the same bed because there is hardly any space.

She used to work as a cleaner at a factory, but she is not currently employed. No one earns in the household, so she survives as she says by 'God's grace', with support from relatives and friends.

The roof of the house is of corrugated iron sheet fixed onto a timber frame, and metal hurricane straps attach the timber wall plate to the concrete block walls. The house needs plastering and painting, but she doesn't have the money. It also doesn't have a latrine, so she uses a neighbour's. 'It's really necessary to finish the house and especially to build a latrine,' she says.

Good-quality materials promote beneficiary satisfaction

Venite Clerilus now lives with her invalid husband and four grown-up children in a retrofitted house which had been partially damaged by the earthquake; the back part had collapsed. She earns a living by buying wholesale small goods such as vegetables and coal, from the countryside and selling them in the city.

The back part of the house was rebuilt, and corner reinforcements and a ring beam for earthquake resistance were added. To allow a future upper floor, reinforcement rods are kept extended beyond the roof, and space retained to add a staircase. With her own funds she also fixed her latrine and built a small septic tank.

The US$1500 she received from Cordaid helped her to make the repairs and retrofitting, using workers trained by Build Change. 'But I wanted to have a concrete roof so that the house can hold up against storms,' she says, and with her savings, and some from her children, she has managed to do that. She still needs to paint the house and is saving money for that.

Venite; her house; and its floor plan.
Source: adapted floor plan from Noll Tufani

1. Bedroom
2. Living
3. Provision for adding staircase and upper floor
4. Corner reinforcements
5. Ring beam joining corner reinforcements
6. Reinforced concrete floor

0   .5   1   2M

Success factors

Owner-driven construction

The key idea driving the owner-driven process was that people do not merely receive a house, but are involved in the design and construction of that house, and gain skills in the process. This process allowed beneficiaries to control the quality of materials to their satisfaction. Technical support by Build Change ensured further construction quality control. By both retrofitting damaged houses and building new houses, the project reached a wider beneficiary group than would otherwise have been possible. Buildings that incorporated hazard-resistant features were made acceptable by using typical Haitian house styles as the basis of the design.

An integrated approach

Instead of only building houses, basic community infrastructure such as paved walkways, drainage, streetlights, and services such as water provision and waste management were integrated into the project. The division and structure of agency roles made this integration possible. Beyond the integration of physical elements, social aspects were also integrated into the project, including land tenure, internal community organisation, capacity building through training, workshops, etc.

In-situ reconstruction

In-situ reconstruction allowed people to continue living where they had existing networks and livelihoods.

Scope for incremental expansion

Allowing for future vertical expansion by providing buildings with the capacity for an extra storey was an effective strategy, given the tight site conditions and growing population.

Community capacity building

Training of local builders ensured houses are earthquake- and storm-resistant, and the skills remain with the community. Additional training to homeowners ensured acceptance of safe building techniques.

Agency partnerships

Bringing together a range of agencies, each with its specialised skills, strengths and resources, greatly contributed to the project effectiveness and success.

Project challenges

Significant challenges included:

- Coordinating timely and effective contributions from a wide range of stakeholders and actors was difficult. Facilitating the alignment of diverse interests from agencies with different backgrounds and cultures added to the complexity.

- While for practical reasons it was easier to concentrate the project inputs in one area, doing so created 'islands of benefit' in a 'sea' of widespread deprivation. This is a common dilemma in many reconstruction projects.
- Although skills training and a cash-for-work program were provided, there was no support for long-term livelihoods and the economic sustainability of the community.
- Apart from the involvement of local authority Casek, the Haitian government was not engaged with the project, leaving leadership and implementation to external agencies. Build Change did succeed in an initiative to build public sector technical capacity: such efforts need to be increased to ensure sustainability after the external agencies leave.

Lessons learnt

This multi-faceted project implemented in partnership between several agencies offers some key lessons:

- By avoiding the typical 'one-size-fits-all' approach on 'greenfield' sites where communities are resettled, this project's in-situ reconstruction approach succeeded in addressing a diverse range of housing needs that would otherwise not have been met.
- The project underlines the significance of an integrated approach, where housing was not built in isolation, but incorporated with community infrastructure such as paved walkways, drainage, streetlights and landscaping, and services such as water supply, latrines and waste management.
- Despite the inherent challenge of coordinating a range of actors, this project demonstrates that a multi-stakeholder and multi-disciplinary partnership between funding agency Cordaid, technical agency Build Change and urban planning support agency AFH, was fruitful in addressing the complexity of the problem. Bringing on board a range of other international partners – IOM and CHF – and the local government authority Casek, maximised the project's potential for success.

In conclusion

Haiti already had widespread impoverishment before the earthquake and had been battered by a cyclone only two years earlier; the earthquake exacerbated the existing conditions of poverty, creating a highly challenging situation. The key elements of the project – hazard-resistant construction, in-situ reconstruction in a highly dense urban informal settlement, partnership between diverse agencies, owner-driven reconstruction and local capacity building – can all pose challenges even in less demanding circumstances, and yet the project was successfully built. This project, with its many positive achievements in a difficult context, is an example of effective post-disaster housing and community reconstruction.

ON THE HILL: A view from Delmas 30.

Earthquake, 2010

Integrated neighbourhood approach

The township of Delmas, which has a population of 350,000 residents, is north-west of central Port-au-Prince. One of its quarters, Delmas 30, grew from the early 1980s as a slum area on a hilly site beside a large ravine. Before the earthquake, conditions and building practices were typical of urban informal settlements in Haiti: very small plots necessitating construction of several floors, often on slopes with no site stabilisation; limited vehicular access, and only to the settlement's edges; internal pedestrian movement by narrow passages, some of them only 50–60 centimetres wide; confined, non-engineered masonry construction with low-grade materials vulnerable to hazards.

Other features typical of Haitian urban informal settlements were also prevalent: high poverty, lack of community infrastructure and services, and vulnerability to public health hazards, notably cholera and malaria epidemics. The large ravine that runs through the settlement was used as an informal waste disposal site; rainwater run-off through the ravine caused flooding and landslides, affecting households living in its lower reaches.

The dense settlement was devastated by the 2010 earthquake, affecting 75 per cent of the quarter's residents and destroying or damaging more than 70 per cent of the 727 houses there. The International Federation of Red Cross and Red Crescent Societies (IFRC) established a large temporary camp in Delmas. This project is an initiative to assist disaster victims to leave that camp and return to their homes.[13, 14, 15, 16]

Why this project case study?

Explicit integration of housing reconstruction with community infrastructure and services makes this project an excellent example of effective reconstruction in the highly challenging circumstances of extensive devastation and widespread, chronic poverty. IFRC's long history of working in the disaster field, the inter-agency partnerships, the development of local skills and capacity, and support for livelihoods were key elements in the project's success.

'My house totally collapsed in the earthquake. I was lucky to survive by crouching in a corner; that saved me.'

– Mary Metoni, Delmas 30, Port-au-Prince, Haiti

INFRASTRUCTURE: Paved walkway with drainage in Delmas 30.

Number of houses built

11 new houses
60 retrofitted houses
200 new or retrofitted houses planned
(Figures are for IFRC only; French Red Cross data unavailable at time of publication)

Implementing agencies
IFRC and Red Cross partners (British, French and Haitian)
Key partners: Build Change; UN-Habitat; PADF; Government of Haiti

Cost
Total US$2.4 million
Cost varied according to house as scope of work varied. One house with 2 rooms, small kitchen and latrine cost US$4620

Donors
IFRC

Context
Earthquake, 2010

Type of post-disaster project
Integrated neighbourhood approach for reconstruction

Location
Delmas 30 (IFRC) and Delmas 9 (French Red Cross), Port-au-Prince, Haiti

Date completed
March 2014

Agency roles

The project was led and implemented largely by the IFRC and its Red Cross partners. The project's broad scope required partnerships between IFRC and agencies including Haitian government agencies – the Ministry of Public Works, Transport and Communications (MTPTC), the National Directorate of Water Supply and Sanitation (DINEPA), the Mayor of Delmas and LGL – and international agencies such as UN-Habitat, Build Change, the Pan American Development Foundation (PADF), the International Organization for Migration (IOM) and Oxfam. Partner agency roles were restricted to advisory support or small components of the overall project.

The French Red Cross began work in Delmas 9 later than IFRC's project in Delmas 30, and used the IFRC project as a template for its own approach. As of May 2013, work in Delmas 9 was focused on housing repair and retrofitting, with plans in place for new house and infrastructure construction and the French Red Cross working in partnership with PADF and Build Change.

The reconstruction process

Before project formulation and implementation, IFRC in partnership with a range of specialist agencies conducted extensive technical studies and problem analyses, including hazard assessment, vulnerability and capacity assessment, surveys of hygiene and sanitation practices, housing studies, including mapping of structural elements, and soil-bearing capacity. These studies were instrumental in informing subsequent project activities.

In order to relocate earthquake-affected households from temporary camps and transitional shelters to the neighbourhoods where they had lived prior to the earthquake, houses were repaired, retrofitted, or rebuilt and a suite of community infrastructure and services were integrated with housing.

Key project features and design aspects

Safer housing

To strengthen housing against the lateral stress typically exerted by earthquakes and hurricanes, repair and retrofitting reinforced the structural frame (beams and columns), added a ring beam, and replaced the roof cover with good-quality corrugated iron sheet. The same principles applied to the construction of new houses. Repairs to some houses were so extensive as to almost amount to building a new house. A partnership with Build Change, an agency specialising in building earthquake-resistant housing, greatly assisted the process.

Footpaths and drainage

Main walkways were covered with pavers made from recycled rubble from the earthquake's debris. An underground drain system was built with concrete cover slabs and grilles for storm water drainage.

Colin Price

Retrofitting, Water and Sanitation Project Manager, IFRC

'Infrastructure is important because everybody in the community benefits from it. Household level water and sanitation is also an important element and we began with retrofitting houses to be able to have access to repair latrines.

'Every house is different and we had to work case by case, but all houses are strengthened against earthquakes and hurricanes. While providing local income from the construction work, we also give on-the-job training on building safer houses. We paint all the houses, providing a psychological boost.'

Britt Christiaens

Project Manager and architect, IFRC

'Community development is the main purpose of this project and we carried out many community studies and focus group discussions.'

Emilie Forestier

Delegate and architect, French Red Cross

'We plan to build or have provision for building two-storey houses because the neighbourhoods are very dense. We have repaired and retrofitted more than 100 houses and this year we will begin building new houses where the earlier houses had been destroyed.'

Emmanuel Pajot

Coordinator, French Red Cross

'This project aims to solve one main problem – poor living conditions – with several components including job training for livelihoods, community health, and infrastructure and housing improvement.

An extensive community consultation process is necessary. We need to go through several steps: first, relocate people to temporary shelters while we repair houses, then retrofit houses against future disasters and finally build new houses.'

SOLAR: Street lights in Delmas 30 use solar power.

Latrines and showers

Damaged latrines were repaired and new latrines built where required. Damaged showers were repaired and, where space was available on the plot, new showers were installed.

Street lights

One hundred solar-powered street lights were installed in public open spaces in Delmas 30. IFRC's community studies revealed that crime and violence took place in dark places, and introducing street lighting helped reduce such activities.

School repair

Two local schools damaged in the earthquake were repaired and retrofitted using safe construction techniques similar to those used in the project housing, allowing classes to return to normal after being run from temporary shelters and under plastic sheeting.

Disaster risk reduction

Specific measures were taken to reduce the disaster risk to the community. People living in low-lying locations in the adjacent ravine were relocated to higher land for safety from flooding; stone retaining walls were built along the ravine to prevent landslides; and people were trained in early warning, evacuation and first-aid.

Livelihood support and capacity building

Each beneficiary household was given a US$250 resettlement grant when leaving the camp and another US$250 unconditional grant three to six months later. In addition to providing desperately needed cash, these grants allowed beneficiaries to revive or start small businesses, and business development training was provided. All construction work was done through small-scale local contractors and construction workers paid by IFRC or its Red Cross partners, injecting further funds into the community. On-the-job training on hazard-resistant construction techniques built local capacity for long-term resilient construction.

WELL-BUILT: Stone retaining wall in Delmas 30. Source: Colin Price.

Marie; her house; and its floor plan.

A small house no barrier to satisfaction

Marie Methanise lives in Delmas 30 in one room of a two-room house that has a small shared kitchen and latrine, and she rents out the front room that has a small veranda. Six people live in her room, including her infant grandchild. Marie earns a living by collecting plastic bottles and selling them for recycling. With the grant from IFRC, she also started a small oil-selling business.

When her previous house on the site collapsed during the earthquake, Marie survived by crouching in the corner. During her almost three-year stay at a nearby camp, IFRC workers discussed with her the rebuilding of her house, and showed her a new house design, which she accepted. She moved back to her rebuilt house in March 2013. 'I benefit from the improved house and the paved road in front of the house. Before, when it rained the road got flooded and it was very difficult to go out,' she says. When asked if she was satisfied, she replies, 'I'm happy with the house, but it's too small. So many of us have to live here, there is no choice. But then, the house was always small.'

1. Front room
2. Veranda
3. Access through narrow alley
4. Bedroom
5. Kitchen
6. Bathroom
7. Concrete block masonry walls
8. Reinforced concrete floor

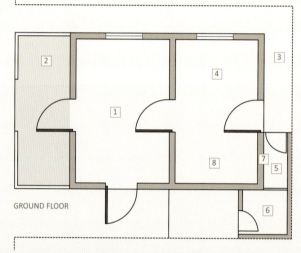

GROUND FLOOR

0   .5   1   2M

Combined housing reconstruction and livelihood support

Viergemene Jean lives in her retrofitted house with 11 other extended family members including her three daughters and their families with children. They live in a typically cramped arrangement in two rooms; having a small veranda in front helps because some of them sleep there at night.

The family members and Viergemene managed to run outside during the earthquake when some of the walls of her house collapsed. She explains that the French Red Cross contracted a local foreman, and he and his workers were shown how to rebuild the house so that it was stronger, and she points to the ring beam, corner columns and hurricane straps. 'They also fixed the latrine at the back and built a shower,' she adds.

Viergemene also received support to revive her small business, selling coal outside her house. She is saving money to paint the walls and add another floor.

Viergemene;
and her house.

Success factors

An integrated approach

The project's integrated approach recognised that housing needs to be a part of a system of infrastructure and services, and backed by community development initiatives, in order to make a liveable neighbourhood. IFRC prioritised repair and retrofitting to resist hazards through in-situ housing reconstruction, building the future resilience of the housing and community infrastructure.

A community-based process

The project was implemented through an extensive community consultation process. A 'Community Platform' consisting of 15 members from locally-based organisations was consulted at all stages of the project.

Local capacity building

On-the-job training of local builders on earthquake-resistant and storm-resistant construction methods allowed not only the building of safer houses, but also increased capacity in the community to construct sustainable and sturdy house construction. By creating construction jobs, it brought income to the chronically poor community when it was needed most.

Extensive experience

The Red Cross movement's extensive experience, global network and access to a range of human and material resources, meant the project was implemented in a professional and carefully considered manner.

Leadership to partner agencies

IFRC was able to provide leadership and maximise contributions from a range of agencies from both the government and NGOs.

The challenges

Haiti with its range of complex political, social and economic issues and history, linked to chronic and deep poverty, is a challenging place to implement such a project as that of the IFRC, so it is understandable that the project would encounter many challenges including:

- In general, a chronic shortage of land made the shift from transitional shelters to permanent housing difficult. Building transitional shelters on plots where houses had been destroyed made that shift more difficult, because the transitional shelters had to be dismantled to make way for new house construction. A long-term strategy for linking the different shelter stages, from temporary to transitional to permanent, would have made this situation less difficult.

- Conflicting interests between the many stakeholders, in particular within the different representative groups in the community, caused delay, with negotiations at times lengthy. IFRC used significant tact to mediate the different interests and achieve consensus, working closely with the Delmas municipality and community leaders.

- Limited government direction meant programs implemented by the large number of international agencies working in Haiti were not coordinated with national priorities. IFRC had to therefore devise its own strategies within this context.

- Lack of waste collection by the municipality means the community dumps waste into the adjacent ravine, with wider consequences: rainwater carries the waste to the city roads and eventually to the sea, affecting the entire environment.

Lessons learnt

The project offers informative lessons on undertaking post-disaster reconstruction in a very poor country such as Haiti, which include:

- The repair and rebuilding of housing within existing neighbourhoods, instead of the 'one-size-fits-all' solutions common in reconstruction projects, allow problems to be addressed in all their complexity.

- The blending of 'top-down' with 'bottom-up', where a high-level and prominent international agency works with an impoverished and marginal community, facilitated an effective reconstruction project.

In conclusion

The extremely difficult context required the strength of a robust international agency such as IFRC in order to implement a housing reconstruction project such as this case study. Nonetheless, the project's achievements could only be realised through partnerships not only with institutional stakeholders, but also with local community-based groups. Although community infrastructure is increasingly being included in post-disaster housing reconstruction projects, here it was done in an explicit and strategic way.

Other notable housing reconstruction projects in Haiti

There are limited examples of permanent housing reconstruction in Haiti, particularly in Port-au-Prince, because of the complexity of land tenure and ownership. There are some scattered projects in rural areas, some of which have been listed as follows;

Community housing development

Implemented in Zoranje after the 2010 earthquake, mainly by the Government of Haiti and the Inter-American Development Bank and their donors, including the Government of Venezuela, Food for Poor and Deutsche Bank. For further information, see:

www.haitilibre.com/en/news-5048-haiti-reconstruction-delivery-of-keys-of-project-of-400-houses-in-zoranje.html (accessed 7 February 2014).

Earthquake reconstruction programme

Implemented in Cap Rouge after the 2010 Earthquake by CRAterre, PADED and Miserior. For further information, see:

CRAterre, *2010 Activities* (report) (Grenoble: CRAterre, 2011).

Neighbourhood housing reconstruction

Implemented in Port-au-Prince after the 2010 earthquake by the World Bank. For further information, see:

http://documents.worldbank.org/curated/en/2013/12/18697368/haiti-port-au-prince-neighborhood-housing-reconstruction-p125805-implementation-status-results-report-sequence-06 (accessed 7 February 2014).

Santo community development

Implemented in Leogane after the 2010 earthquake by Habitat for Humanity and AFH. For further information, see:

http://openarchitecturenetwork.org/projects/santo_community_plan (accessed 7 February 2014).

Notes

1   Blaranova, L. and Christiaens, B., *Project Proposal: Community Development Delmas 30* (Port-au-Prince: IFRC (International Federation of Red Cross and Red Crescent Societies), 2012).

2   United Nations, *Key Statistics: Haiti Relief* (New York: UN Office of the Secretary-General's Special Adviser, 2012).

3   Global Finance (2013) *The World's Richest and Poorest Countries.* Available at: www.gfmag.com/component/content/article/119-economic-data/12529-the-worlds-richest-and-poorest-countries.html#axzz2sW6jNTkP

4   United Nations, *Key Statistics: Haiti Relief.*

5   Lauritzen, E.K., 'The need for integrated rubble management in the aftermath of disasters and conflicts', paper presented at the 6th International i-Rec Conference, Ascona, Switzerland, 2013.

6   Davis, I. (2012) *What Is the Vision for Sheltering and Housing in Haiti?* (report). Available from: http://reliefweb.int/report/haiti/what-vision-sheltering-and-housing-haiti (accessed 12 November 2013).

7   Ibid.

8   *Haiti News*, 'Haiti reconstruction: delivery of keys of project of 400 houses in Zoranje', *Haiti News*, 28 February 2012.

9   CRAterre, *2010 Activities* (Grenoble: CRAterre. 2011).

10 UNHCR, IFRC and UN-Habitat, *Shelter Projects 2011–2012* (Geneva: UNHCR (United Nations Human Rights Commission), IFRC (International Federation of Red Cross and Red Crescent Societies) and UN-Habitat, 2013).

11 AFH, *Community Action Plan for Villa Rosa and Sainte Marie* (Port-au-Prince: AFH (Architecture for Humanity), 2012).

12 Ibid.

13 Blaranova and Christiaens, *Project Proposal: Community Development Delmas 30.*

14 D'Urzo, S., *Supporting Households from the Camp to Community* (Geneva: IFRC (International Federation of Red Cross and Red Crescent Societies), 2012).

15 IFRC, *Haiti Recovery Operation: Summary of the Plan of Action* (Geneva: IFRC (International Federation of Red Cross and Red Crescent Societies), 2011).

16 Rees-Gildea, P. and Moles, O., *Lessons Learned and Best Practices: The International Federation of Red Cross and Red Crescent Societies Shelter Programme in Haiti 2010–2012* (Port-au-Prince: IFRC (International Federation of Red Cross and Red Crescent Societies), 2012).

Tsunami|
Sri Lanka

The 2004 Indian Ocean tsunami struck on the morning of Boxing Day, 26 December. Waves 30 metres high devastated coastal communities in 14 countries, killing 230,000 people.[1] Aftershocks were felt as far away as Alaska.[2] Almost US$14 billion in reconstruction aid was donated from around the world.[3]

Sri Lanka's extensive coastal communities were among the worst hit by the tsunami, second only to Indonesia.[4] More than a million people were affected, more than 35,000 people were killed and almost 150,000 houses were destroyed or damaged. The devastation prompted a large number of housing reconstruction programs by numerous international and national agencies. In addition to the large amount of temporary and transitional housing built, approximately 120,000 permanent houses were planned.[5]

After the tsunami, the Sri Lankan government instituted a 'buffer zone policy', banning new construction in a 100-metre zone from the coastline. The width of the buffer zone was later revised to 35–55 metres, depending on the location.[6] People who had lost homes that were in the buffer zone were resettled in purpose-built settlements inland, and these projects became known as 'donor-driven' because they were built or funded by international donor agencies or international NGOs. People whose homes were damaged or destroyed outside the buffer zone received government grants allowing them to repair their damaged houses or construct new houses in an 'owner-driven' mode.[7]

Because donor-driven resettlement projects progressed slowly, primarily because acquiring suitable land was difficult, the government gave donors the option of implementing owner-driven projects. However, very few donors agreed, mainly because of concerns over the quality of the product, and fear of potential mismanagement and corruption. The UN-Habitat case study that follows is a rare example of an owner-driven project.

Most donor-driven projects were implemented by international NGOs and managed by the donors with local consultants and contracted labour. It was rare to find Sri Lankan NGOs playing a lead role – the Foundation of Goodness (FoG) case study in this chapter, was an exception. The FoG project is also unique because of its long-term approach to engaging with the beneficiary community, maintaining its presence long after most reconstruction agencies had folded up operations after project completion.

◁ AN ISLAND COUNTRY: Sri Lanka has extensive coastal communities.

INLAND: Donor-driven housing in Hambantota New Town, one of the largest post-tsunami resettlement projects in Sri Lanka.

Indian Ocean tsunami, 2004

Community resettlement

The village of Seenigama in the southern district of Galle, near the town of Hikkaduwa, is the base of a local NGO called the Foundation of Goodness (FoG). Following the devastation wrought by the tsunami, FoG received support from national and international donors to rebuild the community, and ran multiple projects that constructed 625 houses and repaired 401 houses in Seenigama and nearby villages. This case study focuses on the largest project in Seenigama – Victoria Gardens.

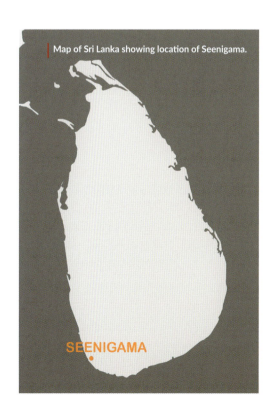

Map of Sri Lanka showing location of Seenigama.

SEENIGAMA

'My wife and two children were washed away by the tsunami. I survived, but couldn't save them; the water was moving too fast.'

– Shanta Siriwardena Arachchige, Seenigama, Sri Lanka

ON THE INDIAN OCEAN: A view from Seenigama showing its coastal environment.

Implementing agencies
FoG

Donors
**Aviva Village: AVIVA-UK; WNS Customer Solutions, Sri Lanka
Perth Village: Perth City Council, Australia
KPMG-LOLC Village: KPMG-UK; LOLC-Sri Lanka
Victoria Gardens: State Government of Victoria, Australia**

Context
Indian Ocean tsunami, 2004

Location
Seenigama village, Hikkaduwa Division, Galle District, Sri Lanka

Number of houses built
153 new houses

Cost
US$80 per square metre

Type of post-disaster project
Resettlement and housing reconstruction

Date completed
December 2007

Why this project case study?

This project is unique in that the implementing agency, FoG, is a local NGO, established through Sri Lankan leadership and situated within the beneficiary community. In most post-disaster housing reconstruction projects, it is common for implementing agencies to be external to the country or based away from the project site.

Agency roles

FoG was founded in 1999 by Kushil Gunasekara, a local of Seenigama. Before the 2004 Indian Ocean tsunami, FoG provided community services such as classes in English and computers, sports opportunities, a maternity clinic and organised the supply of water and electricity from national

service providers to village houses. After the tsunami, in addition to relief and response activities, FoG raised funds to rebuild the devastated communities in Seenigama.

The four 'villages' funded by separate donors were built by different contractors. Victoria Gardens, the largest village, was built by Global Modular Housing Pty Ltd (GMH), a Melbourne-based housing supplier contracted by the Victorian State Government of Australia to design, develop and deliver the project. Initially, GMH was commissioned to engage architects and engineers to plan the new village, and subsequently it was engaged as the managing contractor to deliver the project. The site plan for Victoria Gardens was developed by DPM Consultants, Sri Lanka, led by their Principal Architect, Jayantha Bandara. Various Sri Lankan-based architects, engineers and sub-contractors were appointed throughout the project.

Kushil Gunasekara
Founder and Executive Director, FoG

....

'Seenigama is my village and I have donated my ancestral home, which is now the FoG centre. After the tsunami, seeing that people were being relocated away from their birthplace, I bought land in the village so that housing could later be built for affected villagers here.

We were very careful in beneficiary selection so that people who were seriously affected were selected, and we also checked if they had received a house from some other agency.

All the houses have a garden in addition to the public green areas. I wanted people to have greenery around them and the children to grow up in a natural environment.'

Paskuwalhandi Sampath
Manager of Operations, FoG

....

'I started working at FoG as cleaning and maintenance staff in 2005 after the tsunami. It helped me to learn many new skills, including using the computer and learning English, and to eventually rise to this managerial position.

The house designs here are based on what beneficiaries would prefer. There was a lot of consultation with them. Together with home-based income, FoG has helped people through larger livelihood support – safe coral mining, a brush factory, grocery shops, tuk-tuks, etc.

In the future we will need to focus more on local capacity building instead of giving so much stuff for free.'

Bob Bairstow
Project Manager, GMH, Melbourne

....

'I have nearly 40 years of experience in the construction industry including in roles such as project manager, engineering and construction superintendent and principal engineer. During the Victoria Gardens project, I was the CEO of GMH.

GMH was approached by the Victorian Government to build Victoria Gardens – a planned tsunami reconstruction project. The concept was to recreate a sense of community for the residents located on a single site provided by FoG.

This involved including a community centre, playground, community open space and shops in addition to the 86 houses.'

The reconstruction process

Following the tsunami, FoG purchased land in Seenigama with the intention of providing housing as a way of keeping people from leaving the community. The state of Victoria in Australia funded the Victoria Gardens project, appointing GMH to plan and construct the Victoria Gardens project, while other donors funded the other 'villages'. Beneficiary selection was undertaken by the government, in conjunction with FoG. FoG led the community consultation process to help develop the designs for the housing and for community infrastructure such as the community centre. FoG also provided additional support in the form of extra funding for training and livelihoods, and continues to pay for the maintenance of open areas. The organisation remains in the community as an active agency committed to community development beyond the reconstruction initiative.

Key project features and design aspects

Choice of house design

There were four post-tsunami housing resettlement and reconstruction projects, or villages, implemented by FoG in Seenigama, and house size and design varied across projects. Victoria Gardens is a planned settlement of 84 two-storey duplexes laid out around a central community area. It includes a community centre, a water purification plant, a sewage treatment plant and a playground. Victoria Gardens is FoG's largest resettlement project and is located on newly acquired land. Beneficiaries had lost coastal property and the government's post-tsunami 'buffer zone' policy prevented their resettlement near the coast.

Victoria Gardens beneficiaries were offered several house designs and after significant discussion they selected a two-storey, two-bedroom house design in duplex arrangement. The design provides safety through structurally strong concrete slab and wall construction and an upper floor level above the height of the recent tsunami.

Success factors

FoG's great strength in this project was its ability to empower people, and to continue to do so over a long time frame.

Variety in layout

All four villages have their unique character, each with a clustering of similar houses. In Victoria Gardens, the duplexes have different orientations, external colour schemes and roof shapes, which produce variety within the layout and appearance of the settlement.

Community infrastructure

Paved roads, reticulated power and street lighting, reticulated treated water supply from deep wells, and sewerage are all significant community infrastructure built as part of this housing project.

Structural integrity of houses

Housing was built with a permanent formwork reinforced concrete wall construction system that uses concrete as the formwork within which filler materials are introduced and bonded with the form, so that there is no need to remove the form. Integral floors were built with steel reinforcements run into the wall instead of having the floor structure separate, as is commonly done. Such structures are designed for better resistance against lateral stresses that result from wind, seismic and wave loads, and are significantly superior to the traditional concrete block and concrete frame houses destroyed in the tsunami. Certified Australian-made building materials were used in the wall construction system and for the timber roof trusses.

Maintenance

Unlike most agencies that had implemented post-tsunami housing reconstruction projects and then left the beneficiary community, FoG continued to support the maintenance of its housing projects, consolidating the resilience of the community and housing system.

WELL-PLANNED: A view from Victoria Gardens showing community facilities.

1. Community Centre
2. Playground/Field
3. Water Tank
4. Water Treatment Plant
5. Sewage Treatment Plant
6. Shop

0 5 10 20M

A GOOD PLACE FOR LIVING: Site Plan of Victoria Gardens showing the variety in layout, community facilities and open areas. Source: adapted from Bob Bairstow.

Shantha; his house; and
its floor plan.

Beneficiary pleased with project despite an overcrowded situation

Shantha Siriwardena Arachchige, a resident of Victoria Gardens, lived in a house near the sea before the tsunami washed it away, killing his wife and two children. He was badly hurt, but somehow managed to survive. After the tsunami, FoG conducted a fact-finding mission and selected Shantha and other people who had lived in the 100-metre buffer zone and who were restricted by the government from rebuilding there. FoG showed people models of the different houses; most people liked the two-storey house because they were afraid of another tsunami, and the upper floor provided a place to which they could escape. The houses were distributed by lottery. Shantha moved into his new house in 2007 and remarried. 'Because I had my own home, I could start a new family,' he says.

He was always interested in electronics and communications. He received electrical wiring training from FoG that helped him set up a small shop on the ground floor of his new house where, in an area partitioned off from the living room, he runs his business renting videos, providing computer and photocopying services and recharging mobile phones. With the income from the shop he bought a small communications shop on the main road in Seenigama. He has built an extension to the house, which he rents to pilgrims for further income. 'Without FoG's help, I couldn't have done all this,' he acknowledges.

'This is a good place for living. I am glad that I have some space for gardening and there is a lot of open space all around, which is good for the children as they grow up. When you walk out of the house it's spacious, not cramped,' he says. 'Even if there is another tsunami, we can run upstairs and be safe.'

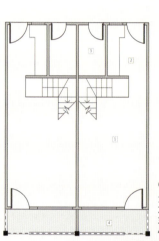

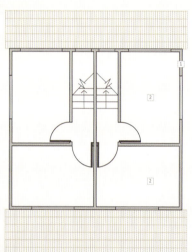

GROUND PLAN

1. Living
2. Kitchen
3. Outdoor bathroom
4. Veranda

FIRST FLOOR

1. Permanent formwork reinforced concrete walls
2. Bedroom

Maintenance encourages acceptance

Sureka Priyanthi lives with her husband and one small child in Victoria Gardens. Before the tsunami she lived with her extended family in a house near the sea. The house was damaged by the tsunami and part of it was then repaired; her parents lived there now. She heard that FoG was going to build houses and so she and her husband approached FoG because there was hardly any space for them in the damaged house. 'I'm happy to receive a house. I'll always be thankful to FoG because they have given us a place to live – a shelter,' she says.

She expresses her satisfaction with the house design: the upper floor has a ceiling, which keeps the heat out; the bathroom is tiled and can easily be kept clean; the drains outside the house keep her compound free of water-logging. She also likes the open area outside her house, which has a playground, community centre and shop.

For Sureka, the most successful aspect of the project is its maintenance. 'FoG employs somebody who maintains the area, cutting the bushes and grass, cleaning the drains and collecting litter from public areas,' she points out. She is also happy about the range of community services offered by FoG: 'Everybody here goes to the FoG centre.'

Sureka; and her house.

Drums for making a living

Gamini Chitna is a traditional dancer and lives in a house in the KPMG/LOLC village with his six-member extended family. The grocery shop he used to have and with which he supported his family was near the seaside and was lost in the tsunami. He has converted part of the living room of his new house to run a small shop, which can be accessed through a window from the front veranda. 'I would like to build a bigger shop outside, because this one takes up space inside the house. I should be able to do that soon, with FoG's help,' he says.

He received livelihood support from FoG in the form of drums and dancing equipment. With that support he's been able to train children, using both the nearby dance academy and his house. 'I'm thankful to FoG. I'm happy to live here with the well-maintained houses, roads and playgrounds,' he says.

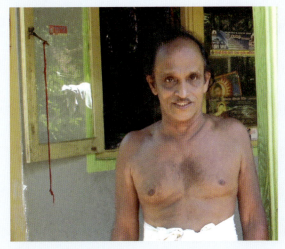 

Gamini; and his house.

Community infrastructure important

Himali Mendis lives with her two children in a house in Aviva Village. Her husband works in Italy to support the family. Her previous house by the sea was totally destroyed by the tsunami, killing her mother. Because her family had been weakened economically, it was very helpful to receive a new house, even if it was smaller than the house she used to have. 'We have a good roof; it protects us from the weather. I like to live in a community like this,' she says.

Himali is particularly happy about the community infrastructure provided by FoG: 'The community centre, library, training centre, playfield – they are all good and successful. My children can read books in the library, play in the playground and attend computer classes.'

The household was given a bicycle as livelihood support. With it, they can move about, buying and selling fish and vegetables. 'My husband used to ride the bicycle, but after he left we still use it,' she says.

Himali; and her house.

The challenges

While there were many achievements in FoG's project, it was difficult matching high design and construction standards to the reality of a country suffering from many years of armed conflict combined with a massive natural disaster. Key challenges included:

- Seenigama is a low-lying coastal area with a high water table. Domestic septic tanks in the AVIVA, Perth and KPMG/LOLC villages often overflow, especially during the rainy season. Victorian Government-funded experts decided to build a sewage treatment plant at Victoria Gardens to replace the use of septic tanks, but due to difficulties managing the system it became necessary to change over to conventional septic tanks and water supply, incurring extra costs. The high water table also meant a water purification plant had to be built.

- Beneficiaries preferred two-storey houses because they were afraid of a future tsunami, but they also preferred detached houses with their increased privacy and space around the house, rather than the more cost-effective duplex housing model.

Lessons learnt

FoG was a unique organisation and its work offers many lessons:

- A 'systems approach', where housing is linked to infrastructure, facilities, services and livelihoods, can help cater to the diverse needs of the affected community.

- Reconstruction projects can also rebuild livelihoods. Livelihood support and training, and development of new job opportunities, were intrinsic to the FoG project, contributing to the overall uplifting of the beneficiary community.

- Strong leadership can achieve positive results. Without Kushil Gunasekara's leadership, this project would not have been possible.

In conclusion

What made FoG unique was its long-term commitment to the development of the community it salvaged after the 2004 Indian Ocean tsunami. The multi-faceted nature of its work saw housing reconstruction sensitively integrated with a wide range of community infrastructure and facilities, livelihood development and local capacity building.

IN THE COMMUNITY: The FOG Centre

Indian Ocean tsunami, 2004

Owner-driven reconstruction

The Hambantota District in southern Sri Lanka was severely affected by the 2004 Indian Ocean tsunami. Together with extensive loss of life and destruction of infrastructure, 1,587 houses were completely destroyed and another 1,606 houses were damaged.[8]

Hambantota was the home district of Sri Lanka's then Prime Minister, Mahinda Rajapakse, and consequently received a significant proportion of recovery aid, with the number of houses built exceeding requirements. The extensive recovery effort was concentrated around the district headquarters town of Hambantota, and outlying areas of the district were less well served.

The division of Tissamaharama, or Tissa, is located on the eastern edge of Hambantota and is less urbanised and more isolated than the central areas of the district. A significant number of poorer and more vulnerable farming and fishing communities had limited resources for recovery.

UN-Habitat took the lead in establishing a contiguous settlement of 218 households named 'Uddhakandara' on about 1.6 square kilometres of land in a rural area in Tissa known as Yodyakandiya. The area was in an elevated inland location and was considered safe for resettlement.

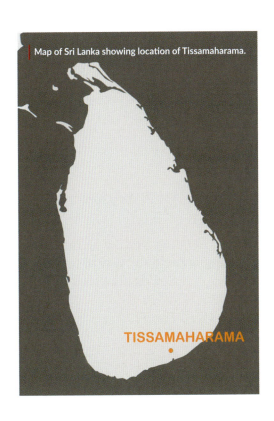

Map of Sri Lanka showing location of Tissamaharama.

TISSAMAHARAMA

'*Luckily I was away with my child at Kirinda market and my husband was at work, so we survived. But when we went back everything we had was gone and the whole area was covered by debris and dead bodies.*'

– **H.G. Nishanti, Tissamaharama, Sri Lanka**

TYPICAL: A mud house in Tissa.

Implementing agencies
UN-Habitat
Key partners: AFH; FAO; GUS

Donors
**UN-Habitat; AFH; Australian Red Cross;
Government of Italy; City of Brescia, Italy; Massa-
Carrara Province, Italy; FAO; GUS**

Context
Indian Ocean tsunami, 2004

Location
**Tissamaharama Division,
Hambantota District, Sri Lanka**

Number of houses built
**157 new houses
61 unfinished houses completed**

Cost
US$4500 for an average 54.5 square metre house

Type of post-disaster project
Owner-driven housing reconstruction

Date completed
Mid-2007

Why this project case study?

This project is a rare example of owner-driven reconstruction in Sri Lanka where the bulk of post-tsunami reconstruction projects are contractor-built. Extensive community facilities have been incorporated into the project, extending it beyond housing reconstruction. The project was implemented through partnerships and offers lessons on multi-stakeholder engagement for future housing reconstruction.

Agency roles

After the tsunami, UN-Habitat initiated an international 'flash appeal' for funding the project and, in addition to its own funds, mobilised funds from various sources including the Australian Red Cross, the Government of Italy and the City of Brescia, Italy. Other funders and partners then came on board, including the Food and Agriculture Organization of the United Nations (FAO), the Human Solidarity Group (GUS), Massa-Carrara Province, Italy, and Architecture for Humanity (AFH).

A number of Sri Lankan organisations provided in-kind and financial support and implemented various project components: among others, the University of Moratuwa provided building materials testing, the Disaster Management Centre provided rainwater tanks and disaster preparedness training, the Sri Lanka Technical College provided training in building trades, Practical Action provided training on construction and enterprise development, the Air Force provided recreational activities, the Industrial Development Board provided training on home-based income generation, the Women's Bank Federation set up a branch in the settlement, Kandalama Hotel provided homestead and roadside planting, the Veterinary Department provided training on goat farming, and Singer provided training on tailoring.

Ibralebbe Abdul Hameed

National Project Manager, UN-Habitat

....

'I have worked in development project management for a long time. Before I worked in UNICEF as Head of Zone Office.

UN-Habitat follows an owner-driven approach in all its projects as it produces better results and more beneficiary satisfaction than donor-driven projects.

Additionally, we provided livelihood options through training and various other inputs that have long-term benefits.'

Aziza Usoof

Architect, and Monitoring and Reporting, UN-Habitat

....

'I am an architect and worked before at Practical Action. Because of my experience, I came to work here on this project.

I provided training on building brick walls using the "rat-trap bond", which makes walls stronger and also creates a cavity wall for cooler interiors.

On-the-job paid construction training was an important part of the project.'

Selvadurai Arumainathan

Planning and Monitoring Manager, UN-Habitat

....

'I worked for a long time at the National Building Research Organisation and have a lot of experience in this field.

About the design of the community centre: it needs more security as it's too open. People can enter at night – taps were stolen from the toilets. We provided 2.5 per cent of the project money as seed funding to the Community Development Councils for maintenance – they will have to find a way to deal with the problem.'

Piyal Ganepola

Deputy Project Manager, UN-Habitat

....

'I was at the National Housing Development Authority and was involved in producing the Guidelines for Housing Development in Coastal Sri Lanka after the tsunami.

The guidelines were followed to ensure standards in this project.

The main driver behind the project was Lionel Hewavasam, UN-Habitat Manager – he almost lived in the community! His recent death has been a big loss.'

The reconstruction process

In the late 1990s, the government's Department of Fisheries and Aquatic Resources initiated a development program in Tissa for settling fishing communities; before the tsunami, 61 households lived in housing that ranged from wattle-and-daub mud construction to brick-and-concrete. Land ownership was formalised and livelihoods supported. Some households were in the process of building a house; most houses were in various stages of incremental construction.

Large tracts of open land were available in Tissa and, after the tsunami, the UN-Habitat program resettled in Tissa 157 households who had lost their homes along the coast. Each household was given a 500 square metre plot and support to build a new house. The existing 61 households were supported to improve or complete their houses.

Project beneficiaries were selected in consultation with the government's Divisional Secretary of Tissa and based on the Division's survey of tsunami-affected households. Funding was channelled through UN-Habitat, which also managed the project through its office in Colombo, with staff deployed to the field.

Houses were built through an owner-driven process. Through initial consultations with the beneficiary community, UN-Habitat's technical team of architects and engineers developed four house designs. After subsequent consultations, the community, represented by the Community Development Councils, agreed on one of the designs.

Household members assisted in the construction of houses, and paid skilled workers were recruited largely from the community, in many cases being those who had received construction training through the project. UN-Habitat staff supervised the construction to ensure quality, and funding was disbursed in stages as each stage of construction was completed satisfactorily.

Basic community infrastructure was provided. UN-Habitat gravelled internal roads and prepared them for bitumen finishing by the governmental Road Development Authority; electricity and water services were arranged from government service providers; drainage channels and culverts were built; a grant from the national Disaster Management Centre supported each household to buy a 5000-litre rainwater tank; and a government bus service was organised. A community centre, designed by AFH, was incorporated into the settlement.

OWNER'S CHOICE: Houses of diverse forms and appearances were built in Uddhakandara through the owner-driven process.

Key project features and design aspects

Owner-driven housing

A standard design for the 157 new houses was developed through an extensive consultation process, the houses being 54.5 square metres with two bedrooms, living room, kitchen and separate structure for a bathroom/toilet. All new house plots were 500 square metres, though varying in shape. The flexible design could be adapted to the needs and preferences of beneficiary households and specific site conditions. Maintaining the minimum house size, households could make internal changes and extensions with their own funds; a choice of building materials was allowed, as long as they were of a quality acceptable to UN-Habitat's technical team; the room layout could be altered according to the site orientation to take advantage of natural ventilation, light and shading; and the roof pitch could be varied. The 61 households originally living in the area received technical support to complete or upgrade their existing houses.

Community facilities

At the heart of the settlement was the community centre designed by AFH. Blending traditional and innovative styles, the three buildings of the centre together comprised a community hall, a primary school, an IT centre, a library, a health centre and an office for the local government authority. Outdoor facilities included a playground, and providing sporting opportunities, in particular, soccer and cricket, and a stadium-like viewing gallery, not previously possible.

Formation of community organisations

As is typical of UN-Habitat projects, a number of Community Development Councils were formed. These were composed primarily of women community leaders and linked together by a Federation of Community Development Councils. The role of the Community Development Councils was to oversee the owner-driven process through 'community contracts' with UN-Habitat, as well as managing savings schemes. Community Development Council members built their capacity in management skills such as book-keeping, accounting and reporting, were entrusted with long-term project operation and maintenance and were provided with 2.5 per cent of the project funds as seed money to sustain the project.

BUILDING FOR THE FUTURE: The community centre.

Success factors

Beneficiary satisfaction

Through UN-Habitat consultations with the beneficiary community, a house design was developed and then adapted by beneficiaries to their needs and site conditions. Beneficiaries, with UN-Habitat assistance, were able to control the construction and monitor the quality of materials. Beneficiary households derived a sense of personalised ownership.

Design innovation

The owner-driven process resulted in a settlement with diverse house designs, in contrast to the typically 'one-size-fits-all' house designs and regimental site planning in many contractor-built post-tsunami reconstruction projects. In addition to the new houses, improvement of existing houses according to their individual stage of construction contributed further to the variety of design.

Community infrastructure and facilities

Unlike many other post-tsunami projects in which reconstructing new houses was the sole project aim, the project involved building a cohesive settlement with a range of facilities and community infrastructure, including internal roads, electricity and water, drainage channels and culverts, household rainwater tanks and a bus service. The community centre catered to community needs – education, health and sports – and served as an important meeting place.

Disaster risk reduction

In this semi-arid region of Sri Lanka, droughts and flash floods are common, and the local soil is prone to rapid swelling and shrinkage. Hazard-resistant standards and structurally sound construction techniques were followed in building construction, assisted by structural testing from the University of Moratuwa. Foundations were built on hard soil by excavating to an adequate depth or being placed on a compacted sand bed; load-bearing clay brick masonry walls were of minimum 200 mm thickness, using a high cement to sand ratio (1:5); and a ring beam was included on top of walls to resist lateral stress from strong winds. In low-lying sites, elevated plinths were built to avoid flooding. The provision of rainwater tanks helped ensure the water supply during droughts and to promote livelihood through gardening.

In addition to such structural disaster risk reduction measures, social initiatives, such as awareness-raising and disaster preparedness training, were also promoted. All houses were insured against natural and man-made disasters, with accident cover for the head of each beneficiary household.

LIFE-SUSTAINING: Rainwater tanks were provided to all the beneficiary households.

Assistance to complete pre-tsunami housing

K.G. Anura lives in Uddhakandara with his wife and two children. He was in the process of building his house before the tsunami, and UN-Habitat supported him to complete it. Through the project he also received training and support for homestead gardening.

He was a fisherman before the tsunami and in 1999 the Fisheries Department gave him a plot of about 500 square metres and US$400 for house construction. The money was only enough to build up to lintel level, and he then borrowed money to build the house to the point where it had a roof but no doors, windows or finishings. He fell into debt, and work on the house stopped. After the tsunami, UN-Habitat supported him to finish the house by giving him US$1800.

'I followed traditional design ideas from my ancestral house where my parents live,' he explains. The house has three bedrooms, a living room and dining room. The toilet, wash area and kitchen are at the back in separate structures.

'I built a large front porch; this is very important in Sri Lanka in the warm climate. We like to sit on the porch and enjoy the breeze, and can receive guests there without disturbing the family.

'I'm happy this place became a settlement. Before it was remote and lonely, and had very few people. Now it's like a village – a community with neighbours and friends.' Before the tsunami there was no water or electricity supply, and UN-Habitat helped have these services connected. 'I'm glad about all the facilities here that benefit everyone; one of my children has started going to the Montessori school here,' he says.

Anura was provided training on business management and supported to build a small hardware shop in front of the house. He was also helped to make a garden and given mango and coconut trees, seeds, plants and gardening equipment. 'You can see how well the garden has grown; we are expecting a lot of fruits to grow here soon,' he says.

Anura and his house.

Beneficiary satisfaction with project layout, design and facilities

H.G. Nishanti lives in a house constructed in Uddhakandara after the tsunami, with her mason husband and three children. The project trained her husband and paid him to work on the construction of their house and other houses in the settlement.

Nishanti used to live in a small seaside house in nearby Kirinda. Luckily the family were not at home when the tsunami struck. They survived, but their house and all their belongings washed away. A few months after staying at a relief camp, they were given a piece of land in Yodyakandiya and money to build a house. 'We liked the house design that was offered and we built our house like that,' says Nishanti. 'We're very happy about the layout of this area. There are lots of facilities and they benefit the community greatly because this is a remote area. We have a lot of freedom here because of the openness; it's not congested like the town. It's good for the children's upbringing because there is a Montessori school here.'

From the different livelihood supports offered, Nishanti chose home gardening. She was given plants, seedlings and seeds, and grows many trees on the homestead, including fruit-bearing ones. Receiving a rainwater tank was useful for storing water for gardening in this dry area. Piped water supply has been provided, but the household still uses water from the tank for bathing, washing clothes and dishes as 'it doesn't cost anything'.

Nishanti; her house; and its floor plan. Source: floor plan adapted from UN-Habitat.

1. Living
2. Bedroom
3. Kitchen
4. Chimney
5. Rendered brick walls
6. Reinforced concrete floor
7. Veranda

0 .5 1   2m

Livelihood support

Coordinated mainly by FAO and GUS, a range of training from building trades to home-based income generation was provided. Because the beneficiaries had mostly been farmers and fishermen before the tsunami, training focused on related livelihood activities. Effort was given to diversifying livelihood options by training for home-based enterprises such as tailoring and basketry, and building skills such as masonry, carpentry, plumbing and electrical wiring. Construction of houses and community facilities involved local workers who were either paid or volunteered, and who gained on-the-job training to develop new skills or to improve existing skills.

Agency partnerships

Successful partnerships between organisations resulted in an integrated community development approach, bridging post-disaster recovery and long-term development. UN-Habitat drew on its extensive experience in housing and infrastructure development; AFH, with its strong global experience, designed the community centre; FAO and GUS brought expertise to support home-based livelihood programs such as gardening, goat farming, tailoring, basketry and mushroom cultivation.

The challenges

In this UN-Habitat project with many stakeholders and actors, challenges inevitably arose in the coordination of the project. These include:

- The construction of roads, drainage and street lighting was the task of the governmental Road Development Authority, and UN-Habitat assisted by levelling and gravelling the internal roads and digging roadside drainage channels in preparation for completion by the Road Development Authority. However, five years after project completion, the Road Development Authority still had not finished all the roadwork, and beneficiaries complained of the difficulty of moving about on muddy roads during the rainy season, and of the flying dust during the dry season. The delay, however, arose because of the limited government resources available in an economically weak country such as Sri Lanka. As one UN-Habitat staff member explained, 'It's only a matter of time when the roads will be completed.'

- The other main challenge has been the maintenance and upkeep of the community centre facilities. Salaries for staff to run the facilities are difficult to find. The buildings, particularly the toilets, lack maintenance. UN-Habitat was unable to contribute further because most of its resources were being directed to post-conflict reconstruction in the north-eastern parts of the country following the end of the conflict in 2009. Given the extensive measures implemented to develop the community's resilience and resourcefulness, over time they should be able to address this challenge on their own.

Lessons learnt

In a context where donor-driven contractor-built projects are predominant, this owner-driven project is unique and offers valuable lessons for future reconstruction projects:

- Even if a project is funded by external donors, it is possible to implement it successfully with the participation of the beneficiary community.

- An integrated community development process is a very successful approach, with post-disaster housing reconstruction coordinated with a diverse group of components to support a range of inter-related activities and outputs.

- In such projects, collaboration and teamwork between different stakeholders – international, governmental, non-governmental, and community – to develop solutions to the multi-faceted problem of reconstruction, are vital.

In conclusion

Owner-driven approaches to post-disaster housing reconstruction are successful in terms of high beneficiary satisfaction and the varied and culturally appropriate built environment that can result. The project was a resettlement and reconstruction project in a politically struggling country that had experienced a massive disaster while in the midst of a drawn-out ethnic conflict. Given such circumstances, it offers valuable lessons on how effective post-disaster housing reconstruction can be implemented even within a context of severe constraints.

Other notable housing reconstruction projects in Sri Lanka

There is substantial literature on donor-driven reconstruction projects in Sri Lanka, though little literature or assessment of owner-driven projects. For further information, see:

Jayasuriya, S. and McCawley, P. (2010) *The Asian Tsunami: Aid and Reconstruction After a Disaster*. Cheltenham: Edward Elgar Publishing.

For an extensive compilation of post-tsunami housing projects in Sri Lanka, see:

D'Urzo, S. (2006) *Towards Sustainability: Building Practices in Post-Tsunami Housing Programmes*. Colombo: GTZ (German Technical Cooperation).

Other projects are:

Eco-village (1)

Implemented in Hambantota after the 2004 Indian Ocean tsunami by Solidarity Sri Lanka (SLS). For further information, see:

http://mams.rmit.edu.au/2ulsye0lkgb5z.pdf (accessed 9 February 2014).

Eco-village (2)

Implemented in Kalutara after the 2004 Indian Ocean tsunami by Sarvodaya. For further information, see:

www.sarvodaya.org/ (accessed 9 February 2014).

Post-tsunami housing

Implemented in Kirinda after the 2004 Indian Ocean tsunami by Colliers International and designed by Shigeru Ban Architects. For further information, see:

www.designboom.com/architecture/shigeru-ban-post-tsunami-housing-for-kirinda-sri-lanka/ (accessed 9 February 2014).

Tsunami safe(r) house

Implemented in Balapitiya after the 2004 Indian Ocean tsunami by Prajnopaya Foundation with design and technical support from the Massachusetts Institute of Technology (MIT) and Harvard University, USA. For further information, see: http://senseable.mit.edu/tsunami-prajnopaya/index.html (accessed 9 February 2014).

Notes

1   USGS (U.S. Geological Survey), 'Magnitude 9.1: Off the West Coast of Northern Sumatra' (U.S. Geological Survey, 2013).

2   ADB, *From Disaster to Reconstruction: A Report on ADB's Response to the Asian Tsunami* (Manila: ADB (Asian Development Bank), 2005).

3   Cosgrave, J., *Synthesis Report: Expanded Summary. Joint Evaluation of the International Response to the Indian Ocean Tsunami* (London: Tsunami Evaluation Coalition, 2007).

4   PreventionWeb (2008), *Tsunami: Data and Statistics*. Available at: www.preventionweb.net/english/hazards/statistics/?hid=71 (accessed 23 October 2013).

5   RADA, *Mid-Year Review: Post-Tsunami Recovery and Reconstruction* (Colombo: RADA (Reconstruction and Development Agency), 2006).

6   Shaw, J. and Ahmed, I.(2010), *Design and Delivery of Post-Disaster Housing Resettlement Programs: Case Studies from Sri Lanka and India*. Available at: http://mams.rmit.edu.au/2ulsye0lkgb5z.pdf (accessed 8 November 2013).

7   Ratnayake, R.M.G.D. and Rameezdeen, R., 'Post disaster housing reconstruction: comparative study of donor driven vs owner driven approach', in Keraminiyage, K. *et al.* (eds) *Post Disaster Recovery Challenges in Sri Lanka* (Salford: University of Salford, 2008).

8   DCS, *Tsunami Census 2004/2005* (Colombo: DCS (Department of Census and Statistics), 2005).

Hurricane |
USA

The Gulf Coast of the USA has a long history of hurricanes. These are becoming more intense and frequent, largely due to climate change. In August 2005, one of the fiercest hurricanes in recent history – Hurricane Katrina – hit the coastal states fringing the Gulf, with physical devastation extending far inland. Hurricane Katrina killed more than 1800 people, injured more than 5000, and inflicted $US108 billion damage to property. It displaced more than one million people and damaged one million housing units, more than half of which were in Louisiana, the worst-affected state, and 220,000 of which were in Mississippi.[1, 2, 3, 4, 5]

Katrina's devastation was so extensive, and the need to rehouse the victims so acute, that reconstruction presented complex challenges in terms of timely delivery and in matching new housing to the needs of the disaster-affected people. In the initial stage, the Federal Emergency Management Authority (FEMA) provided temporary accommodation in caravans locally known as 'FEMA trailers'. These were a short-term solution and in short supply.

Not surprisingly for a disaster in one of the most affluent countries of the world, a multiplicity of agencies and actors initiated reconstruction projects. One of the first permanent housing solutions was the 'Katrina Cottage', designed by architect Marianne Cusato, and constructed in Louisiana and Mississippi. Roughly the size of a FEMA trailer (28.6 square metres), the 'cottage' was built of fibre-cement outer walls, timber framing and metal sheet roofing, and was designed to be wind-resistant and with provision for future extension. Its ease of construction made it a widely adopted housing reconstruction solution.[6, 7, 8]

One widely publicised reconstruction initiative in the Lower Ninth Ward in New Orleans was the *Make It Right* project.[9] It was initiated in 2007 and funded by film actor, Brad Pitt, who invited 21 architects, many of them renowned internationally, to design houses to address reconstruction needs in one of the most ravaged areas of the city. By 2013, 90 of the planned 150 houses had been constructed.[10] These were well-built and energy-efficient. However, as each architect chose a different design template and construction system, thus raising construction costs, these houses were beyond the reach of the low-income community that lived in the area before Hurricane Katrina.

Compared to the *Make It Right* project, other projects had more success in providing affordable housing and incorporating community facilities for the large low-income disaster-affected sector. For example, in Biloxi, Mississippi, Architecture for Humanity (AFH) undertook a similar project to Make It Right, bringing together a number of architects to support reconstruction.[11] Sustaining the housing initiative required the support of locally based organisations. When AFH folded-up their project, the Gulf Coast Community Design Studio continued AFH's work in Biloxi by establishing a base within the community and working with a local community development agency.

The case studies that follow are located in the two most affected states, Louisiana and Mississippi, and present a set of lessons for future rebuilding after disasters. For example, the reconstruction program in Biloxi, Mississippi, is an example of how a team of architects can work collaboratively with a community development agency to contribute to effective housing reconstruction and infrastructure. The Musicians' Village in New Orleans, Louisiana, is an affordable housing project where a community has been rebuilt specifically to nurture the music heritage of the city.

◁ **EXPOSED:** Gulf Coast: Biloxi, Mississippi, hit hard by Hurricane Katrina.

Hurricane Katrina, 2005

Consultative housing reconstruction

The ferocious Hurricane Katrina made landfall on 29 August 2005 and ravaged the Gulf Coast states of the USA. Mississippi incurred the worst property damage, with rapid inundation of 90 per cent of its coastal cities by a 9-metre storm surge invading 20 kilometres inland. More than a million of Mississippi's 2.9 million population were affected, 235 people lost their lives and more than 220,000 houses were impacted.[12, 13]

The devastating winds of Hurricane Katrina and inundation from the huge storm surge caused enormous destruction to the beachfront city of Biloxi in Mississippi. The toll was particularly severe because the city had a large stock of old and weakened housing that was built before hazard-resistant building codes were instituted. Mississippi had the highest rate of low-income households in the USA – more than 42 per cent – at the time of the hurricane. A survey of 6000 households in Biloxi showed nearly all residents lived below

Map of the Gulf Coast showing location of Biloxi.

BILOXI

the national median income level. As a result, 90 per cent of Biloxi households had no flood insurance before Hurricane Katrina which destroyed 80 per cent of the housing stock.[14] Exposing disparities that normally remained concealed, the hurricane hit a vulnerable population, one that could least afford the social and economic costs of the damage and reconstruction.

'After hearing about the hurricane we escaped to our daughter's house in Savannah, Georgia. When we came back, we found our house was gone; we lost everything!'

– **Flora Williams, Biloxi, USA**

SUB-TROPICAL: The project is located in Biloxi's coastal wetlands environment.

Implementing agencies
GCCDS; Hope-CDA

Donors
HUD; Mississippi Development Authority; private donors

Context
Hurricane Katrina, 2005

Location
East Biloxi, Mississippi, USA

Number of houses built
57 new houses
187 rehabilitated houses

Cost
US$750–900 per square metre depending on the amount of volunteer labour

Type of post-disaster project
Reconstruction and rehabilitation

Date completed
2008

Why this project case study?

The Gulf Coast Community Design Studio (GCCDS) was established as an outreach program of Mississippi State University. Led by architect David Perkes, it operates as a team of architects, or 'studio', to respond to the specific reconstruction needs of the Biloxi community.

The GGCDS model has two key aspects:

- designing through community consultation; and
- working in partnership with a community development agency.

This model offers valuable lessons for reconstruction as evidenced by the quality and appropriateness of the housing that was built and the consultative process that enabled the disaster-affected community to recover relatively faster than similarly devastated ones.

Agency roles

The Biloxi housing project was a collaboration between two agencies – GCCDS and Hope Community Development Agency (Hope-CDA). Hope-CDA was a community development agency set-up after Hurricane Katrina to deliver community development programs and to assist low-income communities to access affordable housing. GCCDS and Hope-CDA established offices together in East Biloxi.

The project's first set of houses was built from funds from both private and philanthropic sources. Subsequently, the bulk of funding was provided by the government through the Department of Housing and Urban Development (HUD) and the Mississippi Development Authority.

The reconstruction process

Initial 'case management' was carried out by Hope-CDA and involved identifying potential housing beneficiaries, determining their eligibility, and advising them of options. Even though the focus was on housing, Hope-CDA facilitated a holistic community development package. This included, for instance training in financial management, job skills and home buyer education.

After beneficiaries qualified for housing support, GCCDS worked with each household to design and build a house according to the following principles:

- Consider household structure and needs.
- Match design to budget and site conditions.
- Design with nature by utilising natural light and ventilation.
- Reflect local building traditions.

GCCDS conducted detailed housing damage assessments and prepared topographical maps to understand the extent of house elevation required in specific sites. Designs had to meet revised building regulations that required houses to be elevated above the level of the Katrina storm surge. Technical aspects such as cost-effectiveness, hazard-resistance, energy efficiency and meeting local building codes were also of concern.

Before the hurricane, most people lived in family-owned houses passed down through generations. In the few newer houses – covered by a mortgage and insurance – the insurer reduced or paid-off any remaining mortgage amounts. However, most affected households usually did not have enough money for rebuilding. As a result, Hope-CDA provided

David Perkes
Architect, and Founding Director, GCCDS

'An important aspect of our work has been working with community organisations like Hope-CDA that we share the building with. They do the work to figure out who qualifies for which assistance program, and coordinate volunteers. It was important for us to figure out how to fit within this and how to provide the technical part – the design and construction.

Our focus was to do everything we could to make sure that the people that were going to live in the houses had a real involvement in the process.

Each house was a separate project with its own set of construction documents. None of those projects were stuck with a limited set of plans and we were able to manage that within our technical knowledge and not feel like we were just giving people floor plans.'

Amanda Bauman
Case Manager Supervisor, Hope-CDA

'It's all right here, a one-stop shop. People would come and meet with a case manager, who would determine their eligibility. Then they would stay at the same place to talk with the Design Studio. Since we were sharing a space, it was very easy to walk a few feet to talk to the architect to figure out how everything was going, if any changes need to be made, and so on.

The model was to meet with the homeowner, finding out exactly what they wanted to see in their homes. Yes, it was building houses more resistant to storms, but in addition it was listening to the client and designing according to those conversations.

There isn't one set of blueprints that we used over and over again. We never did two similar houses next to each other.'

these households with a 'forgivable grant' towards the rebuilding of their homes on the condition that they lived in the house for 5 to 10 years depending on funding source. Households that decided to sell or rent their homes had to repay a portion of the grant according to the number of years of full-time occupation. This arrangement acknowledged that people's circumstances may change and thus facilitated flexibility over time.

Key project features and design aspects

Distributed housing
In this project 57 new single-family houses and 187 rehabilitated houses are scattered throughout East Biloxi, with each house designed or repaired according to specific household needs and site conditions. Housing was rebuilt on the existing house sites for homeowners across the city, maintaining the sort of local links and networks that can be a challenge to maintain in greenfield sites where new communities are established.

Consultative design process
Case-by-case consultation on house design and construction with individual beneficiary households allowed the architects to tailor the design to what the families needed and wanted.

Design choices
Householders were able to choose the type and colour of the laminate flooring, floor tiles, appliances, counter tops, cabinets, trim, tiles and finishes, as well as make adjustments to the room layout and positions of window and doors, and to exterior and interior colours.

The architects avoided vinyl siding for external wall cladding and used more durable (and environmentally preferable) timber or composite sidings. Carpeting was avoided because it was unsuitable for a tropical climate and instead laminated timber flooring was used, giving a natural quality.

Climate-sensitive design
The houses were designed to be responsive to the local tropical climate. For example, ceiling heights were up to 2.75 metres instead of a more usual 2.45 metres, to improve ventilation and create a cooler interior as well as provide sufficient height for ceiling fans. Windows were sized and positioned to take advantage of natural breeze and light to make house interiors comfortable and reduce ongoing energy costs. Many of the designs were derived from the traditional 'dogtrot' house with a central breezeway or common space to provide light and ventilation and with rooms on the two adjacent sides. Following local tradition, all houses had large, airy, comfortable balconies or porches. Each house was raised on stilts up to a height of about 5.5 metres to comply with the new building regulations, which created a shaded undercroft space with free air flow.

Flexible grants support changing circumstances

David Wallis, a commercial fisherman, is renting a GCCDS-designed house just across the road from the GCCDS/Hope-CDA office. The original owner had developed lung cancer and had to move to New Orleans for treatment. So he sold the house and repaid a portion of his grant to Hope-CDA. The new owner was renting the house to David, who had moved there in April 2013 with his wife and three children. David's previous house, about 20km away, was destroyed in the hurricane, and he moved to his present location because the rent was affordable.

The house is raised on timber stilts about three metres above ground level to comply with the revised building code. It has three bedrooms, two bathrooms, kitchen and living/dining room, and is accessed with a single-flight staircase going down from the porch. David believes that the house is 'really well-built' as it has two layers of floorboards instead of one to make it stronger, and cross-bracings to prevent vibrations from a nearby railway track. He also appreciates the spray foam insulation under the floor: 'The house stays really cool and I'll save money on the utilities bill,' he says.

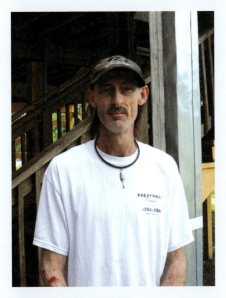

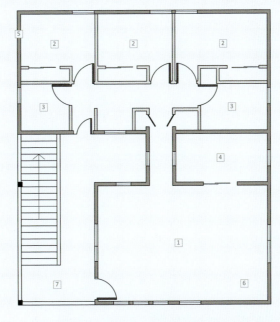

FIRST FLOOR PLAN

1. Living
2. Bedroom
3. Bathroom
4. Kitchen
5. Timber/composite sidings
6. Double floorboards with spray foam insulation beneath
7. Porch

0 .5 1   2m

David; his house; and its floor plan. Source: floor plan adapted from GCCDS.

Respect for the environment

Special attention was given to the sensitive location of the houses within the existing landscape. For example, a significant number of large oak trees in the area survived the hurricane and were retained on site for shade and natural ambience. Each house was specifically designed to fit into its site with minimum site intervention, taking advantage of existing vegetation to frame views from the house and maximise natural cooling and lighting.

Improving house plans through rehabilitation

Most of GCCDS's work in the first two years focused on rehabilitating damaged houses. Many of these were old, often with poorly designed alterations and extensions that had then become the most hurricane-damaged parts of the house. GCCDS rehabilitation included re-design, with spaces re-arranged for better functional performance and future disaster resilience.

Success factors

Consultation

More than any other factor, the extensive consultative design process contributed to the success of the GCCDS project. Through engagement with the end-users, it was possible to meet their needs and provide design services to produce well-designed and appropriate housing.

Disaster risk reduction

All houses followed the revised building codes for wind-resistance and floor heights. Following GCCDS's housing damage assessment and topographical mapping, houses that were assessed as damaged by more than 50 per cent had to be rebuilt. Rebuilt and new houses had to be elevated above the revised Federal Emergency Management Authority (FEMA) base flood level, more than 5 metres in many places because of the huge storm surge inundation. GCCDS assisted people to determine how high they had to build their houses, often increasing the figure to add functionality to the housing. For example, if a house needed to be raised 2 metres, beneficiaries were advised to build the floor a bit higher so that a car could fit under it. Some people were advised to build higher than the base flood level and have extra 'freeboard' (building extra watertight distance between flood level and the house's lowest possible water entry point) to get a discount on flood insurance.

Cross-bracings were added to connect the long posts, contributing to the building's resilience to hurricanes.

Environmental sustainability

Although the budget did not permit building highly energy-efficient houses, an extra US$2000 or so per house was invested for better insulation, with spray foam being used instead of the typical fibreglass batt insulation. Applying insulation under the roof instead of under the attic also provided improved energy efficiency.

Environmental remediation

In addition to its reconstruction work, GCCDS led a project to restore a degraded local wetlands area, Bayou Auguste Neighborhood Wetland Park, as a flood retention area and to minimise future storm surge impact. This was achieved by clearing garbage, re-establishing meandering water channels and restoring local vegetation. The Wetland Park provides habitat for fish and crustaceans, and thus helps with local livelihoods

OWNER-DETAILED: A house with exterior colour of the beneficiary's choice; note the timber sidings used instead of vinyl.

KEPT: Houses were designed to blend in with the local landscape, such as with the oak trees that survived the hurricane.

Flexible grants support changing circumstances

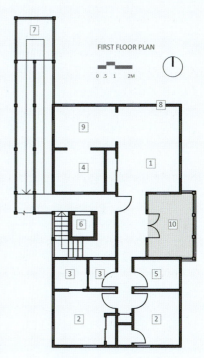

FIRST FLOOR PLAN

0 .5 1 2M

Flora Williams has been a resident of East Biloxi for nearly 40 years. Her old house where she raised four children was destroyed in Hurricane Katrina. Hope-CDA helped her to build a new house designed by GCCDS. She now lives there with her husband, who is elderly and has disabilities.

An architect from GCCDS visited her and discussed what she needed, explaining that the house would have to be raised by 2.75 metres because of the new regulations. Flora then mentioned that her husband was disabled and required special provision. She also wanted a lot of light in the house. 'After the hurricane we used to feel depressed; so I wanted a bright, cheerful house,' she says.

The architect developed a design that included a small lift, as well as an almost 30-metre long ramp in case of power failure during hurricanes. This made the house expensive, so only two bedrooms could be provided. Flora liked the design although she would have preferred a third bedroom, as before, so that her children could stay when they visited. She was able to choose the colours and finishes, and she chose a peach colour, which she really likes.

Flora and her husband moved into the new house in 2007. She really likes it because of the large windows that bring in a lot of light. She also likes the undercroft space and often spends time there. 'It's my favourite part of the house with the nice breeze and all the light for my plants,' she says.

Flora; her house; and its floor plan.
Source: floor plan adapted from GCCDS.

1. Living
2. Bedroom
3. Bathroom
4. Kitchen
5. Laundry
6. Lift for disabled access
7. 30 m timber ramp for disabled access
8. Timber/composite sidings
9. Laminated timber flooring
10. Porch

as well as serving as an important recreational area for the community. The integration of such elements with the housing reconstruction led to a wider set of positive impacts for the disaster-affected community.

Construction by volunteers

The involvement of volunteers saved costs, and their lack of a profit motive helped avoid the substitution of quality specifications with cheaper, less-resilient materials and to ensure quality workmanship. Supervision by GCCDS staff further ensured quality.

Teamwork

The individual specialisations of GCCDS and Hope-CDA were complementary. GCCDS provided building and design expertise, and Hope-CDA provided local community knowledge, client consultation and social support.

Multi-disciplinary team

Although led by architects, GCCDS was multi-disciplinary. For example, a GCCDS engineer developed a friction pile foundation system that allowed a building design based on a minimum soil resistance value regardless of soil conditions. This helped save the cost of soil tests, and was an improvement over more costly concrete pile house designs.

Embedded within the community

GCCDS and Hope-CDA set-up in the heart of the community they served and provided community development and design services, not only for construction of new houses but also for long-term maintenance and repair.

Livelihood support

The project benefited many local building product businesses and tradespersons. Hope-CDA provided training on financial management and job skills for small-scale entrepreneurs. With GCCDS's support, two other community-based partner organisations, Women in Construction and YouthBuild, promoted employment opportunities in the building sector for women and youth and provided on-the-job construction training.

Link with university

There were several benefits to GCCDS being an outreach program of Mississippi State University. In exchange for the expertise and time of university specialists, some of the work brought income back to the University and greatly enhanced its local reputation. Student volunteers contributed to project cost-effectiveness as well as gaining valuable experience for their future careers.

The challenges

Despite the difficulties typical of a post-disaster context, the project was implemented effectively. There were inevitable challenges, including:

- After Katrina, numerous agencies and builders arrived in Biloxi to assist reconstruction. Experienced agencies such as Architecture for Humanity and Habitat for Humanity implemented projects, but there were others that did not have adequate capability. The newly formed GCCDS had to establish its place within this multiplicity of actors, which required commitment and demonstration of credibility.

- Project management was a challenge, with architects, engineers, volunteers, tradespersons and contractors having to work together. Architect David Perkes describes the initial period as 'a completely baffling kind of system of construction'. Eventually the groups learned to work with each other.

- In hindsight, GCCDS realised that additional resilience measures could have been built into the designs. For example, including an adhesive plastic sheet instead of felt in the roof would have made the houses more waterproof because water would not be able to penetrate inside if roof shingles flew off in a strong wind. This feature would have also reduced insurance costs. Later GCCDS house designs were modified in response.

Lessons learnt

The way GCCDS and Hope-CDA implemented the reconstruction project offers valuable lessons such as:

- Architects can play a significant role by using their design skills and capacity for multi-disciplinary work to rebuild houses that specifically meet the needs of households.

- Working in partnerships with groups with complementary expertise greatly improves the capacity to address the multi-dimensional challenges of post-disaster housing.

- Reconstruction projects can address a wide set of community needs through the development of livelihood skills, job creation, supporting local businesses, the restoration of natural landscapes and the training of future professionals.

In conclusion

This project shows how agencies can build upon their individual institutional strengths to address the complex challenges of post-disaster reconstruction. The work of GCCDS in particular highlights the role of the architectural profession in successful housing reconstruction. Teamwork between agencies, in-depth consultation, a base in East Biloxi near the disaster-affected community, the emphasis on local job creation and business development, as well as providing real-world learning for architecture students, are the key positive elements that make this a model housing project with potential replication of the process in disaster-affected areas worldwide.

Hurricane Katrina, 2005

Musicians' Village

The destruction in New Orleans during Hurricane Katrina was mostly due to failure of the embankments along Lake Pontchartrain, unlike other areas closer to the coast where the main impact was from powerful winds. Many low-lying areas were rapidly inundated by rushing water.[15] Populated largely by low-income households, the Lower Ninth Ward was one of the most severely impacted parts of New Orleans.[16]

New Orleans is a city famous for its musical culture, and many of the city's musicians lived in the Lower Ninth Ward. The Musicians' Village project was targeted to address the needs of New Orleans's musicians, and to preserve the musical heritage of the city.

Map of the Gulf Coast showing location of New Orleans.

'My house in the Lower Ninth Ward was destroyed by Hurricane Katrina. A 25-foot wave rushed through my backyard!'

– Smokey Johnson, New Orleans, USA

NOT ONLY HOUSES: The support activities undertaken by NOAHH are broad ranging such as running this thrift shop.

Implementing agencies
NOAHH
Key partners: First Baptist Church of New Orleans

Donors
NOAHH; First Baptist Church of New Orleans; private

Cost
$US100,000 per house
Total cost including elderly duplexes, Children's Park and Ellis Marsalis Center for Music = $US20,726,500

Context
Hurricane Katrina, 2005

Location
Upper Ninth Ward, New Orleans, Louisiana, USA

Type of post-disaster project
Resettlement of disaster-affected households

Number of houses built
72 new houses

Date completed
2008

Why this project case study?

This New Orleans Area Habitat for Humanity (NOAHH) project was one of the few projects in New Orleans that specifically targeted urban, low-income, disaster-affected households by providing affordable housing. The project aimed to build a community rather than simply a group of houses.

Agency roles

Two internationally renowned musicians, Harry Connick Jr and Branford Marsalis, both native New Orleanians, approached NOAHH with the idea of building homes for displaced musicians. NOAHH had identified a large tract belonging to the Orleans Parish School Board for the construction of houses and the idea blossomed into the concept of a neighbourhood and musical hub. NOAHH was impressed with the concept and partnered with them to implement the project.

NOAHH approached the School Board about purchasing the tract of land; the School Board insisted on a bid process and NOAHH was the only bidder, acquiring the land for approximately two-thirds of its pre-disaster appraised value.

Another key partner was the First Baptist Church of New Orleans, led by Pastor David Crosby. The church had planned to build 40 houses in the area under the name of the Baptist Crossroads Project (BCP) a year before Hurricane Katrina. After Katrina, BCP merged with the NOAHH project and, together, they implemented the Musicians' Village project.

Jim Pate

Executive Director, NOAHH

'The main intent was to preserve the musical heritage of New Orleans. Although we had the welfare of the disaster-affected people in mind, this was not a giveaway project. We provide capital, not charity, to our partner families. As in all Habitat projects, we followed the same criteria: need for shelter, ability to pay, and willingness to partner.

However, the houses were built and sold at an affordable cost and the terms of the mortgage were favorable to the homeowners at zero interest rate; the average monthly mortgage payment is US$600; to rent a three-bed house even in that area would be more than US$1000 per month. Most of the homeowners never had anybody in their extended families who owned a house.

The houses were designed by Michael Bell, a local architect, then adapted to the owners' needs for location of rooms, finishes, etc. We followed all the standards to make the houses disabled-friendly, energy-efficient and hazard-resilient. If we knew that somebody needed a ramp, we built it; if somebody became ill and had special needs, we retrofitted the house.'

The reconstruction process

The project was announced at a press conference and publicised through community organisations. Because the project's intention was to create a neighbourhood for musicians, applicants were screened to verify that they were musicians or linked to the music community.

Applicants who did not meet the Musicians' Village selection criteria, but met other needs-based selection criteria, were allocated houses in NOAHH projects in other neighbourhoods. A few families had qualified for a Habitat home prior to the failure of the levees and floodwalls and they were included in the Musicians' Village; however, over 90 per cent of the housing went to musicians.

Because many musicians had informal, untaxed income, often earned in cash, NOAHH took innovative approaches to establish applicant creditworthiness, for example, by accepting diary entries of forthcoming performances. Applicants with outstanding debt or bankruptcy were not accepted. Instead, they received support from NOAHH to improve their creditworthiness and to reapply.

Project houses were provided with a no-interest 20-year mortgage. Each successful applicant household was required to contribute 350 hours of 'sweat equity' instead of a deposit. This included working on the construction of their own or nearby houses – or even performing music for volunteers.

Each monthly instalment includes repayment on the loan principal, land tax, termite treatment and insurance. Monthly repayments are US$500–600, depending on the conditions of particular insurance schemes. For example, households with a scheme that was locked-in without adjustment for inflation had lower premiums.

Key project features and design aspects

Multiple project components

Spread across 3.3 hectares on five city blocks, the Musicians' Village consists of 72 single-family detached houses, five duplexes for elderly residents, the Ellis Marsalis Center for Music and a children's park. The multiple components extend the project beyond the provision of post-disaster housing and contribute to a sense of community.

Single-family houses

The single-family houses are elongated with the narrow façade being the side facing the street in a design derived from the traditional 'shotgun house' of southern USA. Each house is approximately 100 square metres and typically comprises three bedrooms, a living and dining room, and a bathroom with laundry space. People had a choice of seven façades based on traditional patterns, as well as a choice of carpets, counter tops, exterior trim and siding colours, tiles and finishes. They also were able to make small adjustments to the room layout and the position of windows and doors, and paint the interior and exterior with the colours they preferred. Indeed, a key feature of the Musicians' Village has become the variety of colour; many houses were painted in warm, radiant shades.

Duplexes for the elderly

Five duplexes for the elderly were built and rented to elderly or retired residents. The duplexes were grouped facing the street. Each duplex has two residential units with separate entrances. The duplexes followed the Americans with Disabilities Act standards, with four of the units fully compliant, and included features such as 91.5-centimetre doors for wheelchair access, grab-rails and accessible positioning of electrical outlets.

SPECIAL CARE: Front view of duplexes for the elderly.

KEY: The Ellis Marsalis Center for Music.

PLAY THIS: The children's park in the Musicians' Village

1. Ellis Marsalis Center for Music
2. Duplexes for the elderly
3. Children's park

0 10 20   40M

MULTIPLE COMPONENTS: Site plan of Musician's Village.
Source: adapted from NOAHH.

Smokey; his house; and
its floor plan.

A home for an illustrious musician

Smokey Johnson's house in the Lower Ninth Ward was destroyed by the hurricane. Since 2007 he has lived with his wife in a three-bedroom house in the Musicians' Village. Because he is 76 years old and wheelchair-bound, a ramp was built at the back of his house to allow access because the house is built on a high plinth to raise it above flood level.

Smokey is a prominent musician, not only in New Orleans, but internationally; he was the drummer for the famous jazz musician, Fats Domino. He travelled with Domino's band to play music in many countries – Australia, France, Japan, etc. His son is also a musician and plays at a prominent nightclub in the city. By living in the Musicians' Village, Smokey can continue to play and teach music at the nearby Ellis Marsalis Center for Music.

Smokey grows carefully-tended garden vegetables and flowers, a sign of his sense of belonging. 'I'm happy to get this house. This is my home,' he says.

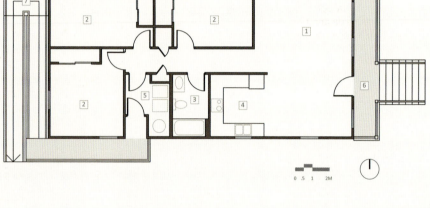

1. Living
2. Bedroom
3. Bathroom
4. Kitchen
5. Laundry
6. Porch
7. Ramp

0 .5 1 2M

Musicians' Village houses resist Hurricane Isaac

Alvin Johnson plays the piano and is a rhythm-and-blues musician. He previously lived in the Lower Ninth Ward and his home was destroyed by Hurricane Katrina's rushing seven-metre high floodwater. He was lucky to be visiting a friend in Mississippi for a barbeque on that day, and so survived.

Alvin says, 'After staying for a few years in different places, I heard that Habitat for Humanity was building a village for musicians. I applied and got this house. I had to work for 350 hours on other houses, which was a great way not to pay a down payment.'

Alvin prefers 'calm' colours, so chose beige and white for the inside and outside of his house. Living in the Village has allowed him to receive training at the Center for Music to improve his skills. He likes the park and on pleasant days goes there to relax with friends.

A year ago, Hurricane Isaac hit the city, but Alvin's house was not affected. There was power outage in the area for a few days, so he stayed with a friend for that time. Upon returning he was pleased to find that everything was all right in the neighbourhood.

Alvin; and his house.

New housing affordable on a low income

Rhonda; and her house.

Rhonda Ford, an owner of a house in Musician's Village, works in various music-related odd jobs – helping make Mardi Gras and other festival costumes, marketing concerts and related events, and contacting musicians. Her children have grown up and left home, though her youngest daughter sometimes stays with her. She is separated from her husband and lives with her taxi driver partner.

At the time Hurricane Katrina struck, she was living at her daughter's house, which flooded and was damaged by 2-metre high water. After two years of temporary accommodation – hotel, church, mother's house, trailer – she moved into her new house.

Rhonda has a low income, but paying a US$506 repayment per month for the house is within her means. She was shown different house models and chose an L-shape design. 'I was pleasantly surprised with the design. You couldn't beat it with a stick,' she says.

Success factors

Contextual design

House designs derived from local New Orleans housing made the houses attractive. The opportunity to select façades, finishes and colours, and to make interior adjustments, allowed residents to personalise their houses and develop a sense of ownership.

Integration with community facilities

Although the focus was on housing – the mandate of Habitat for Humanity – community facilities such as the music centre, residences for the elderly and the children's park allowed the project to expand in scope and provided the amenities that support lively community activities.

Environmental sustainability

Energy-efficient features include: low emissivity glass in windows, low energy water heaters, radiant barrier roof decking for thermal comfort, and spray foam insulation to seal all gaps.

Disaster risk reduction

The project area was flooded after the hurricane, but not to the same extent as the Lower Ninth Ward. With the construction of a new levee nearby, the Upper Ninth Ward was considered a safe place to build. Nevertheless, houses were built more than 30 centimetres above the Federal Emergency Management Authority (FEMA) base flood level, on a raised plinth, on average 1.7 metres above ground level. Houses were built to International Building Code standards for wind-resistant construction. This means that the houses can withstand winds of more than 200 km per hour. When Hurricane Isaac struck in 2012, there was no structural damage to the project houses despite nearly 60,000 houses being damaged across south-eastern Louisiana.

Construction by volunteers

The involvement of volunteers and homeowners (through the Habitat for Humanity construction model) not only saved costs but improved the quality of the built product. This was also because the volunteers and beneficiaries, unlike building contractors, had no profit motive. Qualified architects and engineers supervised to ensure the quality of the design and construction of the housing.

Extensive experience

The extensive experience of the major agencies involved made a strong contribution to the success of the project. Habitat for Humanity has an excellent reputation and global experience in the field of low-income housing. NOAHH has been active in New Orleans since 1983 and has built close to 600 houses in the area as well as repaired about 100 owner-occupied houses.

The challenges

Despite its success, the project faced some challenges including:

- Due to local shortages and high prices, the project used imported Chinese plasterboard that was later found to have a high aluminium and sulphur content and that emitted gases that damaged materials made of copper and posed an alleged health hazard, requiring NOAHH to spend US$55,000 per house on remediation. Residents had to be provided with temporary housing and all plasterboard replaced by a tested local product. Prolonged litigation has followed, where NOAHH is a lead plaintiff on behalf of the homeowners.

- NOAHH provided homeowners with training and a manual on maintenance, but many, being first-time homeowners, were not accustomed to undertaking maintenance activities. Maintenance of natural wear-and-tear is posing a challenge for households on limited incomes.

Lessons learnt

The positive elements of the Musicians' Village project offer the following lessons for housing reconstruction:

- Competent built environment professionals and a humanitarian agency such as NOAHH can work effectively in a team with volunteers and affected communities. Design sensitivity to context and with flexibility for adaptation by users produced satisfactory housing results for all concerned.

- NOAHH managed to achieve a careful balance between not being a charity and yet providing financial advantages to affected communities. The project beneficiaries, while not feeling like recipients of pity, found housing that they could never otherwise have afforded.

- Integration of community facilities, particularly the Ellis Marsalis Center for Music, helped to establish a community and preserve local cultural heritage. To be effective, reconstruction projects often need to go beyond just building houses.

In conclusion

New Orleans had a high poverty rate and significant social disparity before Hurricane Katrina, which the disaster brought into focus. Many of the project beneficiaries, mostly musicians in this city with a vibrant music culture, had low incomes and had lived previously in inadequate housing. The Musicians' Village provided them with well-built houses in a neighbourhood with facilities, safeguarding them from future disasters, and helping the music tradition of New Orleans to continue to flourish.

Other notable post-Katrina housing reconstruction projects

Biloxi Model Home Program

Implemented in Biloxi, Mississippi, after Hurricane Katrina by Architecture for Humanity. For more information, see:

http://architectureforhumanity.org/files/biloxibook_final.pdf (accessed 10 February 2014).

Build It Back Green Program

Implemented in New Orleans, Louisiana, after Hurricane Katrina by Global Green USA. For more information, see:

www.globalgreen.org/articles/global/75 (accessed 10 February 2014).

Make It Right

Implemented in New Orleans, Louisiana, after Hurricane Katrina by the Make It Right Foundation established by actor Brad Pitt. For more information, see:

http://makeitright.org/ (accessed 10 February 2014).

URBANbuild

Implemented in New Orleans, Louisiana, after Hurricane Katrina by Tulane School of Architecture. For more information, see:

www.tulaneurbanbuild.com/index2.php#/home/ and https://tulane.edu/k5/upload/-TCC-booklet-S10.pdf (accessed 10 February 2014).

Notes

1 Bevan II, J.L. *et al.*, *Annual Summary: Atlantic Hurricane Season of 2005* (Miami: National Hurricane Center, 2008).

2 Blake, E.S., 'The deadliest, costliest and most intense United States tropical cyclones from 1851 to 2010 (and other frequently requested hurricane facts)' (technical memorandum) (Miami: National Hurricane Center, 2011).

3 Express Publishing, *Hurricane Katrina: 5 Years and Beyond* (Korea: CKI Inc., 2012).

4 FEMA and HUD (US Department of Housing and Urban Development), *Current Housing Unit Damage Estimates: Hurricanes Katrina, Rita and Wilma* (Denton, TX: FEMA (Federal Emergency Management Authority), 2006), Region VI.

5 Liu, A. *et al.*, *Resilience and Opportunity: Lessons from the U.S. Gulf Coast after Katrina and Rita* (Washington, DC: Brookings Institution Press, 2011).

6 Alter, L. (2008) 'Katrina Cottages rolled out by Lowes nationwide'. Available at:www.treehugger.com/modular-design/katrina-cottages-rolled-out-by-lowes-nationwide.html (accessed 17 October 2013).

7 Lubell, S.,'Lowes makes Katrina Cottages available for purchase'. *Architectural Record Daily News*, 3 November 2006.

8 Stark, J., 'The house that Katrina built', *St Petersburg Times*, 28 January 2006.

9 Feireiss, K. (ed.), *Architecture in Times of Need: Make It Right Rebuilding New Orleans' Lower Ninth Ward* (Munich: Prestel Verlag, 2009).

10 DePillis, L., 'If you rebuild it, they might not come: Brad Pitt's beautiful houses are a drag on New Orleans', *New Republic*, 13 March 2013.

11 AFH (ed.), *Biloxi Model Home Program* (San Francisco: AFH (Architecture for Humanity), 2008).

12 FEMA and HUD (US Department of Housing and Urban Development), *Current Housing Unit Damage Estimates.*

13 Barksdale, J.L., *After Katrina: Building Back Better than Ever* (Mississippi: Governor's Commission on Recovery, Rebuilding and Renewal, 2005).

14 Ibid.

15 Carr, J.H. *et al.*, *In the Wake of Katrina: The Continuing Saga of Housing and Rebuilding in New Orleans* (Washington, DC: Joint Center for Political and Economic Studies, 2008).

16 Logan, J.R. (undated) 'The impact of Katrina: race and class in storm-damaged neighborhoods'. Available from: www.s4.brown.edu/katrina/report.pdf (accessed: 18 October 2013).

Typhoon
Vietnam

Vietnam is one of the five most vulnerable countries in the world to the impacts of climate change.[1] Its long coastline is exposed to a wide range of threats, including typhoons – tropical cyclones – and associated storm surges and flooding. For example, Typhoon Xangsane in 2006 and Typhoon Ketsana in 2009 caused severe devastation, with strong winds and heavy rain accompanied by 2-metre high storm surges that caused extensive inland inundation.[2, 3] Nearly 400 people were killed by these two typhoons and almost 600,000 houses were washed away and destroyed or severely damaged.[4]

Central Vietnam is one of the most disaster-prone areas in the country.[5] It is an impoverished region[6, 7] far from the main cities of Hanoi and Ho Chi Minh City where national development is focused. Agriculture, aquaculture and fishing are the key livelihoods for many, who must then face the wrath of typhoons and floods.

There has been a gradual transition from traditional building materials such as bamboo, timber and thatch, to industrial products such as brick and concrete since the Doi Moi market reforms of the late 1980s.[8] This change in construction processes has not been accompanied either by the production of materials of suitable quality for housing construction or by an understanding of how to build with these materials. For example, 9-centimetre-thin walls made with low-quality brick and slender reinforced concrete posts without a tie beam are common. In many cases, roofs are built with timber framing members running in only one direction, offering less resistance to wind than a two-way framing system. Such houses are easily damaged. Thus, housing is one of the sectors most severely impacted by the frequent typhoons and other disasters in Vietnam.[9]

A subsistence economy in rural parts of the country means many people in Vietnam are not able to afford to build resilient housing, and there is also a lack of skilled professionals capable of building such housing.[10, 11] To address housing vulnerability, it is necessary not only to improve design and construction, but also to train and build local capacity and to provide competent professional support. Government and international NGOs are the main actors in post-disaster housing provision in Vietnam.

Generally, government projects focus on building houses and basic infrastructure – through providing housing loans or subsidies. In many cases these are resettlement projects that relocate vulnerable communities to areas less exposed to hazards. Government projects generally involve little community consultation, few partnerships with NGOs and lack of attention to housing resilience.[12]

International NGO housing projects in Vietnam seek to provide social development and livelihood in addition to housing and basic infrastructure. Projects by NGOs are closely monitored by the government and must be implemented in coordination with the government.

However, signs of change can be noted: For example, the government's '716 Program' was implemented with technical support by the NGO Development Workshop France (DWF). The 716 Program post-flood reconstruction in central Vietnam, which was implemented during 2012–13, successfully reduced disaster risk by building reinforced concrete houses with an upper floor as a safe refuge.[13]

The two case studies that follow are notable examples of housing reconstruction initiatives after Typhoons Xangsane and Ketsana. DWF and Save the Children UK contributed to reducing future typhoon risk by building housing resistant to storms, storm surges and flooding, as well as strengthening community capacity and resilience.

SAFE-REFUGE: A house built in the government's '716 Program'. Source: Tuan Tran Anh.

◁ **DISASTER-PRONE:** A view from coastal Hue, Vietnam, where aquaculture and fishing are common livelihoods.

Typhoon Xangsane, 2006
Typhoon Ketsana, 2009

Housing reconstruction and public awareness

The coastal province of Hue was severely affected by Typhoon Xangsane in 2006 and Typhoon Ketsana in 2009. The extensive construction of vulnerable housing in this area is combined with lack of knowledge on how to build sturdy construction for future disaster events.[14] Therefore strengthening local capacity in building resilient design and construction is essential.

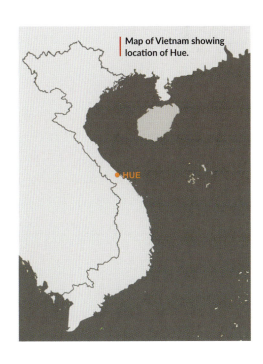

Map of Vietnam showing location of Hue.

HUE

'My house collapsed totally in Typhoon Xangsane. A wave as tall as me came up from the lagoon and washed everything away.'

– Le Xuan Dung, Hue, Vietnam

UNSAFE: Houses such as this in Hue are vulnerable to disasters.

Implementing agencies
DWF)

Donors
ECHO; IFRC; CIDA; Government of France

Context
Typhoon Xangsane, 2006, and
Typhoon Ketsana, 2009

Cost
US$30 per square metre

Location
Thua Thien Hue province (or Hue), Vietnam

Type of post-disaster project
Reconstruction and rehabilitation

Number of houses built
918 houses new or repaired

Date completed
2007, 2010

Why this project case study?

Development Workshop France (DWF) operates in more than 30 countries to develop local capacity in vulnerable communities. It has been working in central Vietnam since the late 1980s. Despite a huge need for disaster-resilient housing, it is one of the few agencies in Vietnam operating with this mandate. Its houses have gained local acceptance because they have proven highly durable during successive typhoons.

DWF has received a number of international and local awards for its work in central Vietnam, including the World Habitat Award (2008), the United Nations Sasakawa Award for Disaster Reduction (2009) and the Hue Province Certificate of Merit (2008).

Agency roles

DWF works in close coordination with the local government authorities known as People's Committees, and its projects are implemented with the support of an established local construction company, Consultants, Designers and Constructors Corporation (CDC), under the Vietnam Government's Department of Construction, further deepening its local connections. DWF is part of a network of development agencies working in Vietnam, and a partner of the Thailand-based Asian Disaster Preparedness Center (ADPC), allowing it to learn from and share with other agencies in the wider region.

DWF then acts as a bridge between the international and local domains in post-disaster reconstruction. Its credibility allows it to access international funds to facilitate housing resilience at the local community level, in Hue. International development agencies that have funded housing reconstruction following Typhoons Xangsane and Ketsana include the European Commission Humanitarian Aid Office (ECHO), the International Federation of Red Cross and the Red Crescent Societies (IFRC), the Canadian International Development Aid (CIDA) and the French Government.

Guillame Chantry

Project Coordinator, DWF

'I've been working in the non-profit sector for more than 40 years and started working in Vietnam with DWF 23 years ago. At that time there were hardly any NGOs here.

Since then, there have been many changes. The economy has grown and Vietnam is becoming a middle-income country, but even then, there is a lack of resources at the local level. For the people here, there are 'everyday disasters', not only big disasters.

Our entry point is housing. That allows us to then support disaster management, climate change adaptation and livelihoods. They're all linked.'

Phan Duc Hanh

Architect, DWF

'We like to visit the communities and meet different people. It's not like sitting in an office in front of the computer all day. We feel happy to help the people in villages to build stronger homes.'

Pham Thi Thien Tro

Architect, DWF

'Architectural education is still too theoretical and can't be applied in reality. A stronger connection to the field is needed; more surveys should be done in villages. Architectural magazines should include articles on this kind of work.

I can talk to different types of people now. I'm more confident. Most importantly, it makes me happy to be able to help the poor.'

Le Tuan Thang

Vice Head, Department of Construction Hue

'I'm trained as an architect and work as an urban planner.

DWF works very closely with us. After Typhoon Ketsana we designed model houses for three areas – coastal, inland plains and mountains. We produced a housing manual and worked with DWF to build these houses. We also worked together to build a safe harbour. We are planning a large housing program with DWF in the future.

DWF staff work directly with the local people and support them to achieve what they need. Working with them has made me understand how to work in these communities.'

Cai Trung Nhu

Vice Chairman, People's Committee of Luc Tri Commune, Hue

'After the typhoons DWF staff came here and did a survey of damaged houses. We helped them to select beneficiaries according to the damage level. Together we held village meetings and prepared the beneficiary list.

In this commune DWF built five new houses and repaired 50 houses. Many other people also wanted help, but the budget was limited, so we helped those who needed it the most.

DWF helped us prepare the Commune Disaster Preparedness Action Plan. This provides directions on what needs to be done by the local authorities and the community during disasters.'

The reconstruction process

DWF has been developing typhoon-resistant housing since the late 1980s. After Typhoons Xangsane and Ketsana, 918 houses were rebuilt or repaired to typhoon-resistant standards, with house floors raised to avoid flooding.

In a process that ensured house designs were acceptable to beneficiaries, DWF architects undertook extensive consultation with individual households and builders to develop house designs based on local housing types. Beneficiaries could choose from shelter designs ranging in size and cost, and could adapt those designs to suit their site and household requirements. No two houses were exactly the same, though all used similar strengthening techniques.

The reconstruction program was combined with an ongoing 'Safer House' campaign that includes training of local builders and teaching safe building principles. Awareness campaigns, animated by songs and folk drama, use mass media such as TV and newspapers, and community gatherings to spread the 'Safer House' message.

DWF also supports disaster preparedness and the developing of early warning systems by providing training and equipment such as sirens and megaphones. By working with the local People's Committees, DWF has enabled each commune or urban ward in Hue to develop its Disaster Preparedness Action Plan, and has supported their uptake through local training and raising community awareness.

Although the main focus of DWF's work in Vietnam is on building and promoting disaster-resilient housing, it also supports wider community development through livelihoods and skills development, microcredit and school education, to strengthen resilience and sustainability. DWF has built safe community facilities and infrastructure including schools, harbours and dykes.

Key project features and design aspects

Ten principles of Typhoon-Resistant construction

DWF projects follow its '10 Principles of Typhoon-Resistant Construction'. Underpinning the 10 principles is the concept that all parts of the building structure are firmly connected to each other to resist strong winds. DWF applies its 10 principles mostly to the single-storey houses commonly found in rural areas of Vietnam. The 10 principles are:

1. Housing should be located on sites not directly exposed to strong wind or that could be flooded.
2. House forms should be simple and have regular shapes so that wind pressure does not have uneven effects due to irregularity of form.
3. Roof slopes should be more than 30 degrees so the roof does not blow off in strong wind, and be less than 45 degrees so that the roof does not crumple in.
4. Roofs should not be extended by more than 80cm beyond the wall, in order to avoid lift-off by wind. Building the veranda roof structure separate from the main roof structure allows the main part of the house to be secure even if the veranda is damaged.
5. The three main parts of the house – foundation, walls and roof – should be securely fastened to each other so that they do not fail at the places where they are joined.
6. The house structure should include bracings and have strong connecting joints between different parts of the house.
7. Roof cover or cladding such as tiles or metal sheets should be securely attached to the roof frame so that they do not fly off during a storm.
8. If the doors or windows do not have shutters, then building similar openings on the opposite side of the house will let the wind flow through the house without creating wind pressure inside that could make the house collapse.
9. Where possible, doors and windows should be able to be closed, with strong doors and windows with latches.
10. Existing trees around the house should be retained, and if absent then new trees should be planted, to create a barrier to wind. Trees with deep roots are best and should be planted at a safe distance to avoid damage by broken branches.

In additional, DWF houses are built on a raised plinth of 1–1.5 metres, made of brick and concrete to be waterproof.

Success factors

Local relevance

DWF's 10 principles are based on local building practices and local hazards. They apply specifically to the houses in central Vietnam and are locally relevant. They are improvements to existing building techniques to overcome weaknesses.

Design consultation

Instead of following a 'one-size-fits-all' approach, DWF caters to each beneficiary household through intensive consultation to develop house designs that are in tune with beneficiaries' needs and preference, and this results in local acceptance.

Design as a two-way process

DWF's initiative is a two-way process – DWF's knowledge of typhoon-resistant construction is derived from the specific hazards confronting central Vietnam been shaped by local building materials and construction – knowledge which in turn is transmitted back to the local context.

Demonstration effect

The fundamental mandate of building resilient housing as exemplified in DWF's 10 principles is not compromised in the consultative process. This project is built on experience gained over a long time, where local communities gradually learns to appreciate and accept the merits of DWF's principles through DWF-built housing's demonstrable good performance over many disaster cycles.

Easily understandable concepts

Because they are rooted in local practice, DWF's design principles are easily understood and applied by local builders with some basic training, replicated by others.

Multi-disciplinary team

DWF employs a range of professionals, such as architects, engineers, social workers and community animators, who work together to address the multi-faceted problem of promoting and building resilient communities.

Integrated approach

Although the focus of the project is on promoting resilient housing, that housing is integrated with development initiatives including livelihood support, disaster risk reduction, building schools and harbours, and community infrastructure such as dykes and culverts for flood protection.

Long-term engagement

That DWF has operated in Vietnam for more than two decades testifies to its organisational success. While it is common for agencies to fold-up their operations after completing reconstruction projects, DWF remains embedded in the local context and has maintained its presence in central Vietnam for an extended period to continue consolidating community resilience.

Yen; her house; and its floor plan.
Source: floor plan adapted from DWF.

Yen does not fear typhoons

Mai Thi Yen lives with her husband and two children in a DWF-built house in Le Thai Thien village, Luc Tri commune, Hue. Both Yen and her husband fish for a living in the large lagoon behind their house. They used to live in a small flimsy house which completely collapsed in Typhoon Xangsane. Many houses in the village were affected and most lost their roofs. Because Yen and her family lived right next to the lagoon, they were hit by the storm surge and everything was washed away.

DWF supported them after the storm to build a durable and resilient house. Yen had lost her fishing boat in the typhoon, and DWF gave her a new boat and fishing nets, enabling her family to recover its livelihood. Yen expresses her gratitude: 'Before we didn't have the money to build a strong house and we suffered. DWF has saved us.'

In this village, DWF built seven new houses to replace houses that were totally destroyed, and repaired and strengthened five more houses. The new houses have floors raised at least a metre above the ground to avoid floods. A dyke was built along the lagoon to protect the village from flooding, and culverts allow water flow. In addition to strengthening physical resilience, DWF raised awareness and capacity in the community. As Yen says: 'Because of this project, we came to know people at the Commune People's Committee. Now my husband is a member of the local Flood and Storm Committee and he has received training on using warning equipment; he goes from door to door to warn people if there is a typhoon threat.'

After Yen's new house was built, she added a timber mezzanine floor as a storage loft. Two years after the house was built, Typhoon Ketsana hit. The loft then came in handy; the family took shelter there and escaped from the storm surge. Yen's house withstood the strong winds, did not suffer any damage and was proven resilient, resulting in further acceptance of DWF's work. Yen says, 'I feel comfortable and safe that I no longer live in a flimsy house and don't have to worry about typhoons.'

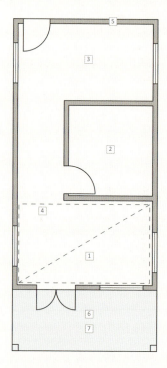

1. Living
2. Bedroom
3. Kitchen/Dining
4. Loft above
5. Brick walls
6. Reinforced concrete floor raised 1.5 m to avoid flooding
7. Veranda

Good-quality materials promote beneficiary satisfaction

Le Xuan Dung lives with his wife and three children in a DWF-built house in Le Thai Thien village, Luc Tri commune, Hue. He used to live in a boat as a mobile fisherman and he settled in Le Thai Thien village in 2000 after a large flood when the government made this a resettlement area for affected fishermen. He could only afford to build a temporary type of house, and it was completely destroyed in Typhoon Xangsane.

After the typhoon, DWF supported him by building his new house and giving him a boat and fishing nets, because he had lost all his fishing equipment. The house has a sturdy structure with steel angles running end to end on the roof to prevent the metal sheets from lifting off in strong wind. Steel hooks and wire are used to securely fix the roof cladding to the purlins. All the doors and windows have latches to secure them during a storm. The house has a reinforced concrete floor on a plinth raised 1.25 metres above the ground to protect the house from floods. The area he lives in, near a large lagoon, experiences regular flooding. 'We live together with the floods for three months every year, but at least they don't enter the house,' says Dung.

Three years after Typhoon Xangsane, Typhoon Ketsana hit, but the house experienced no damage, even though there was a 1.5 metre high storm surge. Many houses in the village were damaged, but not those built by DWF. 'The life of my family has become stable. We no longer have to worry about typhoons and floods,' says Dung.

'When DWF built my house, I got training on safe house construction. Even if I can't build a house myself, I now understand what makes it safe,' he says, adding, 'I received more training to become a member of the Commune's Flood and Storm Prevention Committee and I know about the Commune Disaster Preparedness Action Plan.'

Dung; and his house.

The worry-free mind of a trained builder

Doan Van Cu is a local builder in Le Thai Thien village, Luc Tri commune, Hue. He has a sturdy house which survived in Typhoon Xangsane in 2006. He later built a kitchen extension at the back, but that collapsed when Typhoon Ketsana hit in 2009.

After Typhoon Ketsana, DWF ran a training program for local builders on safe house construction and Cu took the training. He then repaired and strengthened his house. He added four 2mm steel angles on the roof to keep the roofing sheets secure, and he strengthened the connecting joints in the structure. 'After I repaired my house I have no fear of storms. I can go to work with a worry-free mind,' he says. Cu's wife used to fish in the nearby lagoon, and after the typhoons DWF supported her livelihood by providing new fishing nets.

'If DWF again builds houses in this area, they might ask me to do the work because I am now trained and have experience from repairing my own house,' Cu says.

Cu; and his house.

Local partnerships

Working closely with the local People's Committees enables DWF to operate in Vietnam, where the government strongly monitors the activities of foreign agencies. It also allows the local authorities to have a stake in the project, to extend a helping hand, and to provide technical support through a local construction company and the government's Department of Construction, which further facilitates ownership by local stakeholders.

International links

DWF's links with prominent international development agencies facilitates the funding of its projects, especially for reconstruction after disasters, the successful implementation of which then strengthens its international reputation.

The challenges

The challenges identified below are concerned with the long-term nature of DWF's work:

- Despite DWF's connection with different networks and being in this arena for a long time, replication or adaptation of DWF's concepts has been limited and DWF remains largely unique. Given the frequent disasters in Vietnam, and the large numbers of people affected, the need for resilient housing is immense. The resources that a small organisation like DWF can access are less than optimal. It is therefore important that the lessons offered by DWF are shared extensively for wider uptake by a large cohort of development agencies, as well as the government.

- DWF's 'Safer House' campaign, the training of builders and the uptake by local communities remains small in scale: 918 houses repaired or built where nearly 600,000 were impacted by Typhoons Xangsane and Ketsana. An important question is whether DWF would be able to retain its community outreach and local relevance if it grew into a large organisation. Would it then distance itself from the communities with which it has such a strong connection?

- Were DWF to leave, how would locals continue with the initiative? It is important to begin developing local organisations that are able to provide future leadership.

Lessons learnt

The long-standing experience of DWF offers a set of lessons, including:

- The application of simple, but sound, technical principles, such as DWF's 10 principles, can contribute to resilience of housing to disasters.

- Working closely over a sustained period with local stakeholders and at-risk communities helps gain local acceptance and support.

- Operating on multiple levels – international, national and local – allows an organisation to build useful bridges between those levels, leading to a range of productive partnerships. International credibility enables funds to be accessed.

- Integrated development can be incorporated in housing projects by including the improvement of community infrastructure, livelihood support and the training of local builders.

- Using local building materials and labour supports the local economy and livelihoods.

In conclusion

DWF's work offers valuable lessons for building resilient communities in Vietnam and the wider disaster-prone Asia-Pacific region. The work highlights the impact that can be achieved through projects that combine practical training for local builders and built environment professionals with a range of technical and developmental inputs including community infrastructure and facilities, livelihood support and raising awareness for building safer homes.

TALKING THROUGH ISSUES: Consultation with beneficiaries was a key aspect of DWF's work. Source: DWF.

Typhoon Xangsane, 2006
Child-centred housing reconstruction

The coastal city of Danang, the largest in central Vietnam, is exposed to fierce typhoons which are increasing in frequency and intensity due to climate change. On 1 October 2006, the city was devastated by Typhoon Xangsane, one of the strongest cyclones in the last 40 years.[15] More than 70 people were killed, nearly 500 people injured, and 320,000 houses were destroyed or damaged.[16, 17, 18] Many houses totally collapsed and a large number lost their corrugated metal sheet roofing. The extensive damage caused by very strong winds was compounded by a 2-metre-high storm surge, inundating large areas of land.

| **AFTER:** Devastation to housing by Typhoon Xangsane in Danang.

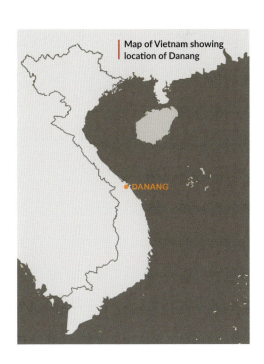

| Map of Vietnam showing location of Danang

DANANG

'The brick walls of my house fell in Typhoon Xangsane and killed my mother.'

– Nguyen Thi Anh, Danang, Vietnam

VERANDAH ADDED: The SCUK houses had a provision for adding a front verandah, which beneficiaries had built themselves.

Implementing agencies
SCUK
Key partners: CACC; DWF

Donors
ECHO; SCUK

Context
Typhoon Xangsane, 2006

Location
City of Danang, Vietnam

Number of houses built
88 new houses
419 house roofs repaired

Cost
US$1200 for a 34 square metre house

Type of post-disaster project
Reconstruction and repair

Date completed
2007

Why this project case study?

Save the Children UK (SCUK) has been working in Vietnam since 1990, and its focus is child-centred development. Typhoon Xangsane, which impacted central Vietnam in 2006, revealed the highly vulnerable nature of the housing stock and how that vulnerability adversely affects the well-being of children and families. SCUK decided to implement this housing reconstruction and repair project, the first of its kind for the agency.

Despite lack of experience in the housing reconstruction area, the SCUK project was implemented in a professional manner with inputs from Development Workshop France (DWF) and a local consulting firm, Central Architecture Consulting Company (CACC), both of which have significant experience in designing and building typhoon-resistant housing.

Agency roles

SCUK has been operating in Vietnam since 1990 with offices based in Hanoi and Ho Chi Minh City. Its work focuses on child care and protection, primary education, child-focused HIV/AIDS prevention, and disaster preparedness and response. It works closely with the Committee for Population, Family and Children (CPFC), which is the leading governmental body dealing with child welfare and rights in Vietnam. In this project, SCUK also worked closely with Danang's Department of Construction for approval and monitoring of the housing design and construction. The project was implemented in close coordination with the Danang People's Committee, the governmental municipal authority.

Because of its long experience in the field of typhoon-resistant housing, DWF, based in nearby Hue, was engaged to provide technical support. DWF conducted four training courses for local consultants, builders, community leaders and beneficiaries, and provided technical advice during construction. A Danang-based architectural firm, CACC, was contracted to produce the design and specifications in coordination with DWF.

The bulk of project funding was provided by the European Commission Humanitarian Aid Office (ECHO), supplemented by 16 per cent funding from SCUK.

Nguyen Thanh Binh

Architect, and Vice-Director
CACC, Danang

'Our consulting company works on a range of design projects for different clients including several NGOs such as SCUK. In this project, my main concern was to design and build strong wind-resistant houses. I had to make sure that the design provided simple solutions that were easy to apply here and at the same time made the houses storm-resistant. It was also important that the cost was reasonable.

I had to go from house to house; you can't have the exact same solution for each house. In this way I learnt about the community. I feel happy to be able to help poor people build a strong house. I feel good when I meet them.'

The reconstruction process

Soon after the typhoon, a joint rapid assessment mission was undertaken by the Disaster Management Working Group consisting of members from SCUK, ECHO and other NGOs and government agencies. The assessment covered the needs of different sectors, including food security, infrastructure and health, and disaster risks. In particular, it found that the poorest households were stretched to the limit coping with the aftermath of the typhoon, and that there was an urgent need for housing

reconstruction. ECHO then came to an emergency decision to begin the immediate recovery of the disaster-affected community in Danang, providing funds to SCUK to implement the project.

SCUK undertook more detailed assessments of the most severely impacted communities and selected beneficiary households that were the most vulnerable, particularly those with children experiencing serious hardship. All beneficiary households had children, many with disabilities.

Even though a large number of houses were destroyed or damaged by the typhoon, the aim of the project was to target intervention to support the most vulnerable households, particularly those with small children, and at the same time disseminate resilient design and construction concepts. Through the project, 88 houses that had collapsed were reconstructed using typhoon-resistant construction methods, and roofing was repaired on 419 houses. Housing designs and specifications were prepared by the architectural firm CACC, which then contracted local builders, and managed and supervised construction.

The project also focused on a school, repairing toilets, restoring electricity, providing electric fans, in all benefiting more than 1,000 children. Two pre-schools were also repaired, and 5,000 children who were at risk of dropping out of school were provided with school uniforms to encourage them to continue their schooling.

DWF training sessions contributed to local technical understanding and community awareness on improved typhoon-resistant design and construction.

| REHABILITATED: A pre-school in the SCUK project.
| Source: Nguyen Thanh Binh.

A sense of security

Nguyen Thi Anh lives with her husband and a child in a house built through the SCUK project. She and her husband run a small street-side stall for selling noodle soup. When Typhoon Xangsane hit, her previous house collapsed, killing her mother. Because she had an infant and was homeless after the typhoon, SCUK built her a new house.

Three years later, when Typhoon Ketsana struck, Anh was very frightened because the house was near the coast. She fled with her family to a relative's house further inland. When she returned, she found the house intact and undamaged. 'My previous house had thin walls and collapsed in the typhoon, but this house has thicker and stronger walls. I feel safe and comfortable living in this house,' she says.

Anh has built a small front veranda, and an extension at the rear of the house. Even though she has a small family, she often has visiting relatives, so she needs the extra space. The front veranda is a local tradition, a shaded open space for relaxation and other household activities in the hot, humid climate. 'All the SCUK homeowners have now added a veranda,' she says.

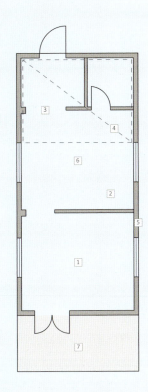

Anh; her house; and its floor plan. Source: adapted floor plan from Nguyen Thanh Binh.

1. Living
2. Bedroom
3. Kitchen/Dining
4. Loft above
5. 150 mm brick walls
6. Reinforced concrete floor
7. Paved area can be converted to front veranda

0 .5 1   2m

Key project features and design aspects

Flexible design

The 34 square metre house design of the SCUK project consisted of two main rooms – a living room in the front leading to a bedroom, with a bathroom and kitchen at the back of the house. A paved area, 4.0 metres by 1.8 metres, in front of the house could be converted by the beneficiaries to a verandah by building a roof over it. In this way the verandah structure was kept separate from the main house structure, and the house could remain safe in a typhoon even if the verandah was damaged.

Resilient housing

To build a sturdy house resilient to future typhoons, the design included: 15 centimetre-thick brick walls instead of the typical 9 centimetre walls that were vulnerable to typhoons; three continuous reinforced concrete bands at the top, middle and bottom of walls, to impart lateral strength against strong wind; concrete rainwater gutters at the two ends of the house to prevent the metal sheet roof cladding lifting off in strong winds; a loft or reinforced concrete mezzanine floor slab for greater strength; and two L-channel metal angles running transversely from end to end on each of the two roof slopes to further secure the metal sheet cladding.

DWF design principles for typhoon-resistant construction were followed (see previous case study), such as strong connections between different parts of the house, avoiding a shallow roof pitch and not extending the roof eaves too much. Having a steeper roof pitch for wind-resistance allowed a loft to be included. Lofts provided safe refuge in the event of storm surges or floods, and valuable belongings could be kept dry there.

Success factors

Site planning and building design

Although the houses included measures for typhoon-resistance, their layout and appearance followed local house designs, allowing them to fit into the local context and gain the acceptance of beneficiaries. The building materials, such as brick, concrete, and metal sheeting, no different to those used in local houses and available locally, were used in an improved way for greater housing resilience.

Disaster resilience

The main emphasis in this project was on building disaster-resilient housing. When Typhoon Ketsana struck in 2009, the project houses were unaffected, clearly demonstrating their resilience.

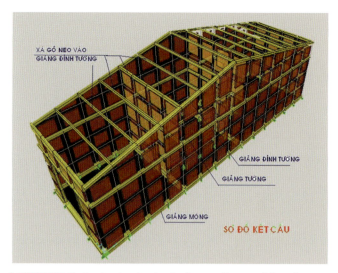

STRENGTH : Design drawing showing the three continuous reinforced concrete bands that contribute to the house's typhoon-resistance. Source: Nguyen Thanh Binh.

DANGEROUS BUILDINGS: Thin brick walls were common, making houses vulnerable to typhoons.

SECURED: Metal angles on the roof protect the roofing sheets against strong wind. Source: Nguyen Thanh Binh.

Ease of construction

Because the SCUK house design was based on local design patterns and local building materials, it was easy for local builders to construct. DWF ran one-day training sessions, enough for local builders and construction workers to grasp the concepts of typhoon-resistant construction.

Cost-effectiveness

Including typhoon-resistant elements increased housing costs by an estimated 8–10 per cent, an amount easily offset by not incurring repair or rebuilding costs from future typhoon damage.

Housing as part of a larger package

In addition to housing reconstruction and repair, other child-centred disaster recovery project elements included the repair of, and provision of new facilities for, a school and two pre-schools, and distribution of school uniforms to encourage school attendance.

Partnership with DWF

The project gained significantly from the partnership with DWF, providing training, technical support, and valuable experience in typhoon-resistant design and construction in the central Vietnam region. This partnership also served to disseminate the worthwhile work of DWF more widely in the central Vietnam region.

Other local partnerships

By working closely with government agencies, including the People's Committee, Department of Construction and CPFC, SCUK was able to operate effectively in Vietnam where the government carefully monitors the work of external agencies. Engaging a local architectural company, CACC, brought local design knowledge, contributed to the local economy and included another important local stakeholder, as

well as providing the means for beneficiaries to seek post-construction support, for example, the repair of small leaks. CACC fulfilled its role in a highly professional manner, as noted in ECHO's monitoring reports.[19]

International links

SCUK's international status, with operations and chapters in many parts of the world, allowed access to funding and resources from international sources.

The challenges

As in most housing projects of this kind, there were also challenges, some of which are not only specific to this project, but apply also to other projects in Vietnam that aim to build community resilience in the reconstruction process:

- While the houses built under this project demonstrated disaster-resilience, the bulk of houses destroyed by the typhoon were reconstructed following the same design and construction methods that had made them vulnerable in the first place – recreating risk. Little has been done by local authorities post-project to promote the concept of disaster-resilient housing. Such housing construction principles need to be adopted and enforced at the national level in a legal and professional framework.

- At 34 square metres, the project houses were small, particularly in a context where large extended families are common, and most beneficiaries built extensions which generally did not follow typhoon-resistant design principles, placing their owners at risk. Nevertheless, the strongly built SCUK 'core-house' provides safe refuge even if extensions are damaged.

Lessons learnt

The SCUK project was implemented with significant technical inputs to impart typhoon-resistance to the housing built. It offers a set of key lessons:

- Resilient housing can support the well-being of children by providing them and their families a safe place to live.

- Local acceptance of new housing designs can be assisted by improving on existing design and construction practices rather than supplanting them with unfamiliar designs, and at the same time ensuring that new houses fit into the local context.

- The involvement of competent built environment professionals, in this case from CACC and DWF, can result in highly professional project implementation, with good quality, durable housing being built.

- Combining housing with a larger educational infrastructure package can help address the schooling needs of children and contribute to their long-term development.

- Using local consultants, building materials and labour supports the local economy and livelihoods, contributing to sustainable development.

In conclusion

This project highlights a key dimension of resilience – the way in which housing can support the welfare of children, serving as an investment in future generations. When backed by competent design and technical expertise, prioritising the safety of children in post-disaster housing projects will ensure a better life for those children. The project demonstrates that dedicated and skilled architects are able to make valuable contributions to the post-disaster housing reconstruction field.

Other notable housing reconstruction projects in Vietnam

716 Program

Implemented in seven Central Vietnam provinces after floods in 2011 by the Government of Vietnam. For more information, see:

http://english.vietnamnet.vn/fms/government/70999/pm-agrees-to-expand-support-for-families-threatened-by-floods.html (accessed 11 February 2014).

Community-designed safe housing

Implemented in Danang after Typhoon Xangsane by the Center for International Studies and Cooperation (CECI) and the Asian Disaster Preparedness Center (ADPC). For more information, see:

www.adpc.net/v2007/programs/udrm/promise/INFORMATION%20RESOURCES/Safer%20Cities/Downloads/SaferCities19.pdf (accessed 11 February 2014).

Flood-/storm resistant shelter

Implemented in seven Central Vietnam provinces after Typhoon Ketsana by Vietnam National Red Cross (VNRC). For more information, see:

www.ifrc.org/docs/appeals/09/MDRVN00609.pdf (accessed 11 February 2014).

Typhoon Ketsana disaster recovery

Implemented in Quang Nam province after Typhoon Ketsana by Habitat for Humanity Vietnam. For more information, see:

www.habitatvietnam.org/Website_Files/3.%20Where%20We%20Build/Quang%20Nam.pdf (accessed 11 February 2014).

Notes

1 Dasgupta, *S. et al.*, 'The impact of sea level rise on developing countries: a comparative analysis', World Bank Policy Research Working Paper 4136. (Washington, DC: World Bank, 2007).

2 Minh, H.B. and Crimmins, C. (2006) 'Typhoon Xangsane, flood toll reaches 169', in *Reuters on Reliefweb*. Available at: http://reliefweb.int/report/viet-nam/typhoon-xangsane-flood-toll-reaches-169 (accessed 5 September 2012).

3 World Vision, *Typhoon Ketsana: One Year Anniversary* (Hanoi: World Vision Vietnam, 2010).

4 CCFSC (Central Committee for Flood and Storm Control) (2013) *Disaster Database*. Available at: www.ccfsc.gov.vn/KW6F2B34/Co-so-du-lieu-thien-tai.aspx (accessed 22 October 2013).

5 Nhu, O.L. *et al.*, 'A preliminary analysis of flood and storm disaster data in Vietnam', in *Global Assessment Report on Disaster Risk Reduction* (Geneva: UNISDR (United Nations International Strategy for Disaster Reduction), 2011).

6 Anh, V.T., 'Uncovering regional disparities in poverty in Vietnam using CBMS data', *CBMS Network Updates*, VI (2009): 3.

7 IFAD, *Enabling Rural Poor People to Overcome Poverty in Vietnam* (Rome: IFAD (International Fund for Agricultural Development), 2010).

8 Norton, J. and Chantry, G., 'Vaccinate your home against the storm: reducing vulnerability in Vietnam', *Open House International*, 33 (2008): 2.

9 MoNRE, *National Target Program for Climate Change Response* (Hanoi: MoNRE (Ministry of Natural Resources and Environment), 2008).

10 ADPC (Asian Disaster Preparedness Center), 'Promoting safer housing construction through CBDRM: community-designed safe housing in post-Xangsane Da Nang City', *Safer Cities*, 19 (2007).

11 Norton and Chantry, 'Vaccinate your home'.

12 Anh, T.T., 'Developing sustainable housing options for disaster-prone regions of central Vietnam', PhD thesis in progress, Melbourne, RMIT University, 2013.

13 VietNamNews (2013) 'PM agrees to expand support for families threatened by floods'. Available at: http://english.vietnamnet.vn/fms/government/70999/pm-agrees-to-expand-support-for-families-threatened-by-floods.html (accessed 31 October 2013).

14 ADPC, 'Promoting safer housing construction through CBDRM'.

15 Ibid.

16 Ibid.

17 CCFSC, *Disaster Database*.

18 Minh and Crimmins (2006) 'Typhoon Xangsane, flood toll reaches 169'.

19 Brouant, O., *Rebuilding a Safer Future for Families Affected by Cyclone N6 Xangsane in Central Vietnam* (project appraisal worksheet) (Brussels: ECHO (European Commission for Humanitarian Aid Office), 2006).

PART III
Conclusion

Lessons from the case studies

'With a little extra money people could have a roof on the house and know that after the next storm they won't have to go up and fix the roof. I know that it sounds like a technical thing, but when it's multiplied many times, it can have a big impact on the community.'

– **David Perkes, Architect, GCCDS, USA**

URBAN CHALLENGE: Rebuilding a community takes more than good house design.

What is sustainable reconstruction after natural disaster?

The 12 projects discussed in Part II – implemented in different geographic contexts by a range of agencies – show the great diversity of sustainable post-disaster housing reconstruction. They demonstrate approaches to building community resilience through housing when responding to bushfire, cyclone (also called hurricane or typhoon), earthquake and tsunami. More than resilient building products, success here results from linking these physical products to a wider set of social and institutional processes. While resilient designs and construction methods have been known for quite some time, implementing them on the ground is often extremely challenging, and it is the effort put into addressing these challenges that sets these projects apart.

Challenges

- *Community capacity:* For disaster-affected households, rebuilding and maintaining houses with improved and resilient construction methods presented difficulties, especially when communities did not have prior experience in building. Technical support from the implementing agencies did, in most of the cases, overcome this. Nevertheless, community capacity remains a key area for attention in future housing reconstruction.

- *Quality control:* The quality of construction and building materials in post-disaster circumstances is often a challenge, and most of the implementing agencies had special measures such as supervision and monitoring to ensure standards were met. However, when agencies had not implemented a disaster-resilient design project before, they could only learn from mistakes made in early stages of the project.

- *Urban challenges:* Cities, and particularly urban informal settlements, presented challenges of land supply and tenure

◁ MORE THAN HOUSING: Support for livelihoods makes housing reconstruction more effective.

for reconstruction projects. Several of the cases studies revealed the role of the government to be quite limited when clearly land supply and tenure are a key governmental responsibility. Similarly, provision of public services, again typically a government role, was lacking in some cases, which undermined projects' success. Another challenge in the urban context was that the complexity of reconstruction in urban areas necessitated the engagement and coordination of a large number of stakeholders.

- *Replicability and upscaling:* A key question, articulated by a staff member of one of the implementing agencies in Haiti, is: 'Are we creating islands of benefit in a sea of widespread deprivation by such projects?' The case study projects do indicate possible future directions for effectiveness in rebuilding after a disaster, but there is yet much to be done in widely replicating and scaling up their successes.

- *Sustainability of investments:* Questions arise around the long-term sustainability of projects built in areas exposed to climate change impacts. Also, whether the legacy of skilled external agencies will be replicated and sustained locally. Extensions and changes will be made to the reconstruction housing – who will ensure that these will be built to resilient standards? In wealthier countries building regulations provide a safeguard, but in the majority of countries in the world such regulation is usually lacking.

- *Long-term support:* As has been argued in most of the case studies, creating resilient housing reconstruction is not only about building new houses, but also about supporting it with community infrastructure and facilities. However, without the implementing agency having a continuing presence in the project area, problems can arise when the responsibility for the long-term maintenance and functioning of such facilities is handed over to the community.

Key successes and lessons

Notwithstanding the above challenges, the case study projects offer a set of valuable lessons for effective post-disaster housing reconstruction. While some of these lessons were context-specific, there were also many that had wider relevance.

- *Integration of housing with community infrastructure:* A key message that runs throughout the book is that post-disaster housing reconstruction must not be merely building new houses to replace those damaged, but must rather be an integrated approach where a range of other elements are provided, particularly community infrastructure and facilities such as roads, water, sanitation, electricity, schools, community buildings and parks. The Integrated Neighbourhood Approach (INA) project of the IFRC in Haiti does this explicitly, but most of the other projects also incorporate community infrastructure. In Australia and the USA, because of the existing high level of public services and infrastructure, this was not a key undertaking of the implementing agencies; nonetheless in the temporary villages in the Australian projects, community infrastructure, including roads, utilities, playgrounds and community buildings, was a vital element, even when built for the short term.

- *Support for livelihoods and the local economy:* The opportunity to earn a living, that is a livelihood, is essential for those affected by disaster. Throughout discussions with disaster-affected communities during fieldwork for this book, the regeneration of livelihoods was emphasised as being as great a need as housing; in many of these communities, the house is also a workplace for home-based livelihoods. Most of the implementing agencies supported livelihoods as part of their housing reconstruction initiatives, through mechanisms such as skills training, provision of equipment, the necessary infrastructure for a livelihood, start-up supplies, or through cash-for-work. In addition, the reconstruction projects supported local economies through the creation of jobs and marketing opportunities for a range of local building products suppliers and producers.

- *Sustained engagement:* Instances where organisations such as FoG in Sri Lanka, GCCDS in the USA and DWF in Vietnam continued to work in the reconstructed community, expanding programs into wider community development, building upon success, were particularly effective in addressing challenges of replicability, upscaling and long-term support. Such approaches must be taken up more widely by agencies in the future.

- *Multi-stakeholder engagement:* The complexity of post-disaster housing reconstruction is reflected in the involvement of a wide range of stakeholders and professionals in all the case study projects, a key reason for their effectiveness. This is a paradigm that can be expected to grow in significance over the future as disasters become more complex and the global forces of climate change and urbanisation continue to create unprecedented challenges.

- *Role of built environment professionals:* Within the multi-stakeholder engagement paradigm, it was found that built environment professionals played a significant leadership role because the effective design and construction of housing and community infrastructure is central to post-disaster reconstruction. The projects of BRAC, DWF, GCCDS and SCUK demonstrated the valuable role played by architects and also supporting the capacity building of future professionals through the involvement of students and young professionals.

- *Owner-driven approach:* Several case study projects demonstrated the value of the owner-driven approach – BDRCS in Bangladesh, Cordaid in Haiti and UN-Habitat in Sri Lanka – leading to, foremost, beneficiary satisfaction.

Even where agencies played a stronger role, community consultation and participation indicated success, such as in the projects of BRAC in Bangladesh, GCCDS in the USA and DWF in Vietnam. While owner-driven projects might have some drawbacks such as long implementation time and difficulty of quality control, these were shown to be overcome through technical support by implementing agencies. While in the past owner-driven projects were rare, the success of projects such as these case studies points the way forward to more widespread application of this approach.

- *Success in difficult contexts:* Even in difficult contexts, such as those with high poverty or remoteness of location, well-designed and innovative projects are able to achieve success. The projects in Haiti were such examples in a highly impoverished country, and the projects in Bangladesh were also so in addition to being implemented effectively in very remote areas.

The above lessons are drawn from extensive empirical field-based research across six countries and 12 case studies that examined on the ground the performance and outcomes of post-disaster housing reconstruction projects globally, as well as institutional policy and practice in this field. This book should serve as a useful guide to agencies acting in the reconstruction field to understand some of the core issues in the field and how they might be better addressed. In a world beset by an increasing spectre of tragic disasters, by understanding the needs and context of disaster-affected communities, strengthening professional capacity and integrating housing with a range of vital elements, post-disaster reconstruction can serve as a vehicle to protect people and property over the long term and establish resilient and sustainable communities.

'We will always be thankful to the people who have given us a place to live – a shelter.
We have all what we need here – school, library, training centre, playfield. I like living here.'

– Sureka Priyanthi, Foundation of Goodness beneficiary, Seenigama

BENEFICIAL OUTCOMES: Life after sustainable housing reconstruction in Seenigama.

Bibliography

ADB (2005) *From Disaster to Reconstruction: A Report on ADB's Response to the Asian Tsunami*. Manila: ADB (Asian Development Bank).

ADPC (Asian Disaster Preparedness Center) (2007) 'Promoting Safer Housing Construction Through CBDRM: Community-designed Safe Housing in Post-Xansane Da Nang City', *Safer Cities*, 19.

AFH (2012) *Community Action Plan for Villa Rosa and Sainte Marie*. Port-au-Prince: AFH (Architecture for Humanity).

AFH (ed.) (2008) *Biloxi Model Home Program*. San Francisco: AFH (Architecture for Humanity).

Alter, L. (2008) 'Katrina Cottages Rolled Out by Lowes Nationwide'. Available at: www.treehugger.com/modular-design/katrina-cottages-rolled-out-by-lowes-nationwide.html (accessed 17 October 2013).

Anh, V.T. (2009) 'Uncovering Regional Disparities in Poverty in Vietnam Using CBMS Data'. *CBMS Network Updates*, VI(3).

Anh, T.T. (2013) Developing Sustainable Housing Options for Disaster-prone Regions of Central Vietnam. PhD thesis in progress. Melbourne, RMIT University.

Barksdale, J.L. (2005) *After Katrina: Building Back Better than Ever*. Mississippi: Governor's Commission on Recovery, Rebuilding and Renewal.

Battenbough, G. (2009) 'Nineteen Firms Unveil Bushfire Designs', *Architecture and Design*. Available at: www.architectureanddesign.com.au/news/industry-news/nineteen-firms-unveil-bushfire-designs (accessed 1 April 2014).

BDRCS (2011) *Early Recovery Response for Cyclone Aila Affected Most Vulnerable People of Khulna District, Bangladesh* (project proposal). Dhaka: BDRCS (Bangladesh Red Cross and Red Crescent Societies).

Bevan II, J.L. et al. (2008) *Annual Summary: Atlantic Hurricane Season of 2005*. Miami: National Hurricane Center.

Blake, E.S. (2011) 'The Deadliest, Costliest and Most Intense United States Tropical Cyclones from 1851 to 2010 (and Other Frequently Requested Hurricane Facts)' (technical memorandum). Miami: National Hurricane Center.

Blaranova, L. and Christiaens, B. (2012) *Project Proposal: Community Development Delmas 30*. Port-au-Prince: IFRC (International Federation of Red Cross and Red Crescent Societies).

Brouant, O. (2006) *Rebuilding a Safer Future for Families Affected by Cyclone N6 Xansane in Central Vietnam* (project appraisal worksheet). Brussels: ECHO (European Commission for Humanitarian Aid Office).

Building Commission (undated) *A Guide to Building in Victoria After the Bushfires*. Available at: www.weepa.com.au/_dbase_upl/guide_building_bushfires.pdf (accessed 1 April 2014).

Bushfire CRC (Cooperative Research Centre) (2009) *Victorian 2009 Bushfire Research Response* (Final Report, Chapter 5: Integrative Studies). Available at: www.bushfirecrc.com/sites/default/files/managed/resource/chapter-5-integrated-studies.pdf (accessed 1 April 2014).

Carr, J.H. et al. (2008) *In the Wake of Katrina: The Continuing Saga of Housing and Rebuilding in New Orleans*. Washington, DC: Joint Center for Political and Economic Studies.

CCFSC (Central Committee for Flood and Storm Control) (2013) *Disaster Database*. Available at: www.ccfsc.gov.vn/KW6F2B34/Co-so-du-lieu-thien-tai.aspx (accessed 22 October 2013).

Cosgrave, J. (2007) *Synthesis Report: Expanded Summary. Joint Evaluation of the International Response to the Indian Ocean Tsunami*. London: Tsunami Evaluation Coalition.

CRAterre (2011) *2010 Activities*. Grenoble : CRAterre.

Dasgupta, S. *et al.* (2007) 'The Impact of Sea Level Rise on Developing Countries: A Comparative Analysis', World Bank Policy Research Working Paper 4136. Washington, DC: World Bank.

Davis, I. (2012) *What is the Vision for Sheltering and Housing in Haiti?* (report). Available at: http://reliefweb.int/report/haiti/what-vision-sheltering-and-housing-haiti (accessed 12 November 2013).

DCS (2005) *Tsunami Census 2004/2005*. Colombo: DCS (Department of Census and Statistics).

DePillis, L. (2013) 'If You Rebuild it, They Might Not Come: Brad Pitt's Beautiful Houses are a Drag on New Orleans'. *New Republic*, 13 March 2013.

DHS (Department of Human Services) (2013) *Victorian Bushfire Appeal Fund Progress Report and Financial Information*. Available at: www.dhs.vic.gov.au/bushfireappeal/about-the-fund (accessed 1 April 2014).

D'Urzo, S. (2012) *Supporting Households from the Camp to Community* (PowerPoint presentation). Geneva: IFRC (International Federation of Red Cross and Red Crescent Societies).

EM-DAT (2013) *The International Disaster Database*. Available at: http://imgur.com/a/KdyTV#0 (accessed 15 April, 2014).

Express Publishing (2012) *Hurricane Katrina: 5 Years and Beyond*. Korea: CKI Inc.

Feireiss, K. (ed.) (2009) *Architecture in Times of Need: Make It Right Rebuilding New Orleans' Lower Ninth Ward*. Munich:, Prestel Verlag.

FEMA and HUD (US Department of Housing and Urban Development) (2006) *Current Housing Unit Damage Estimates: Hurricanes Katrina, Rita and Wilma*. Denton, TX FEMA (Federal Emergency Management Authority), Region VI.

Fire Recovery Unit (2013) *Victorian Bushfire Recovery Four Year Update*. Melbourne: Department of Planning and Community Development.

Flinn, B. and Beresford, P. (2009) *Post-Sidr Family Shelter Reconstruction Bangladesh*. London: Department for International Development (DFID).

FPP (Forest Peoples Programme) (2009) 'Cyclone Aila's Devastation of the Bangladesh Coast – Another Victim of Climate Change?' Available at: www.forestpeoples.org/region/bangladesh/news/2010/10/cyclone-aila-s-devastation-bangladesh-coast-another-victim-climate-ch (accessed 25 October 2013).

Global Finance (2013) *The World's Richest and Poorest Countries*. Available at: www.gfmag.com/component/content/article/119-economic-data/12529-the-worlds-richest-and-poorest-countries.html#axzz2sW6jNTkP

Haiti News (2012) 'Haiti Reconstruction: Delivery of Keys of Project of 400 Houses in Zoranje'. *Haiti News*, published 28 February 2012.

Hong Kong Red Cross (2009) *Bangladesh Cyclone Aila: Work Report 1*. Hong Kong: HKRC.

IFAD (2010) *Enabling Rural Poor People to Overcome Poverty in Vietnam*. Rome: IFAD (International Fund for Agricultural Development).

IFRC (2010) *Bangladesh: Cyclone Aila. Final Report*. Geneva: IFRC (International Federation of Red Cross and Red Crescent Societies).

IFRC (2011) *Haiti Recovery Operation: Summary of the Plan of Action*. Geneva: IFRC (International Federation of Red Cross and Red Crescent Societies).

Jha, A. *et al.* (2013) *Safer Homes, Stronger Communities: A Handbook for Reconstructing after Natural Disasters*. Washington, DC: World Bank.

Kabir, R. (2009) *Post Cyclone Sidr Family Shelter Construction in Bangladesh: Documentation of Plans and Processes*. Dhaka: UNDP (United Nations Development Programme).

Lauritzen, E.K. (2013) *The Need for Integrated Rubble Management in the Aftermath of Disasters and Conflicts* (PowerPoint presentation). Paper presented at the 6th International i-Rec Conference, Ascona, Switzerland.

Liu, A. *et al.* (2011) *Resilience and Opportunity: Lessons from the U.S. Gulf Coast after Katrina and Rita*. Washington, DC: Brookings Institution Press.

Logan, J.R. (undated) 'The Impact of Katrina: Race and Class in Storm-damaged Neighborhoods'. Available at: www.s4.brown. edu/katrina/report.pdf (accessed 18 October 2013).

Lubell, S. (2006) 'Lowes Makes Katrina Cottages Available for Purchase'. *Architectural Record Daily News*, 3 November 2006.

Minh, H.B. and Crimmins, C. (2006) 'Typhoon Xansane, Flood Toll Reaches 169', in *Reuters on Reliefweb*. Available at: http://reliefweb.int/report/viet-nam/typhoon-xangsane-flood-toll-reaches-169 (accessed 5 September 2012).

MoNRE (2008) *National Target Program for Climate Change Response*. Hanoi: MoNRE (Ministry of Natural Resources and Environment).

Nhu, O.L. *et al.* (2011) 'A Preliminary Analysis of Flood and Storm Disaster Data in Vietnam', in *Global Assessment Report on Disaster Risk Reduction*. Geneva: UNISDR (United Nations International Strategy for Disaster Reduction).

Norton, J. and Chantry, G. (2008) 'Vaccinate Your Home Against the Storm: Reducing Vulnerability in Vietnam'. *Open House International*, 33(2).

NSW Government (2011) *Supporting Secondary Dwellings (Granny Flats)* (fact sheet). Sydney: Department of Planning and Infrastructure.

Parliament of Victoria (2010) *Final Report: 2009 Victorian Bushfires Royal Commission*. Melbourne: Government Printer for the State of Victoria.

PreventionWeb (2008) *Tsunami – Data and Statistics*. Available at: www.preventionweb.net/english/hazards/statistics/?hid=71 (accessed 23 October 2013).

QUT (Queensland University of Technology) (ed.) (2010) *Impacts and Adaptation Response of Infrastructure and Communities to Heatwaves: The Southern Australian Experience of 2009*. Gold Coast, NCCARF (National Climate Change Adaptation Research Facility).

RADA (2006) *Mid-Year Review: Post-Tsunami Recovery and Reconstruction*. Colombo: RADA (Reconstruction and Development Agency).

Ratnayake, R.M.G.D. and Rameezdeen, R. (2008) 'Post Disaster Housing Reconstruction: Comparative Study of Donor Driven Vs Owner Driven Approach', in Keraminiyage, K. *et al.* (eds) *Post Disaster Recovery Challenges in Sri Lanka*. Salford: University of Salford.

Rees-Gildea, P. and Moles, O. (2012) *Lessons Learned and Best Practices: The International Federation of Red Cross and Red Crescent Societies Shelter Programme in Haiti 2010–2012*. Port-au-Prince: IFRC (International Federation of Red Cross and Red Crescent Societies).

Seraj, S.M. and Ahmed, I. (2004) *Building Safer Houses in Rural Bangladesh*. Dhaka: Bangladesh University of Engineering and Technology (BUET).

Shaw, J. and Ahmed, I. (2010) *Design and Delivery of Post-Disaster Housing Resettlement Programs: Case Studies from Sri Lanka and India*. Available at: http://mams.rmit.edu.au/2ulsye0lkgb5z.pdf (accessed 8 November 2013).

Siddik, M.A. *et al.* (2012) *Cyclone Sidr and Housing Sector*. Saarbrucken: Lambert Academic Publishing.

Standards Australia (2009) *Construction of Buildings in Bushfire-prone Areas* (AS 3959-2009). Sydney: Standards Australia.

Stark, J. (2006) 'The House that Katrina Built', *St Petersburg Times*, 28 January.

Tran, M. (2012) 'Bangladesh Villagers Still Struggling After Cyclone Aila's Devastation', *The Guardian*, 6 March.

UNDP (2005) *Fix the Risk* (documentary video). Dhaka: UNDP (United Nations Development Programme).

UNHCR, IFRC and UN-Habitat (2010) *Shelter Projects 2009*. Geneva: UNHCR (United Nations Human Rights Commission), IFRC (International Federation of Red Cross and Red Crescent Societies) and UN-Habitat.

UNHCR, IFRC and UN-Habitat (2013) *Shelter Projects 2011–2012*. Geneva: UNHCR (United Nations Human Rights Commission), IFRC (International Federation of Red Cross and Red Crescent Societies) and UN-Habitat.

United Nations (2012) *Key Statistics: Haiti Relief*. New York: UN Office of the Secretary-General's Special Adviser.

USGS (U.S. Geological Survey) (2013) 'Magnitude 9.1: Off the West Coast of Northern Sumatra'.

VBRRA (2011) *Legacy Report*. Available at: http://trove.nla.gov.au/work/159343996?selectedversion=NBD51051068 (accessed 31 March 2014).

Victoria Police (2009) *Bushfire Death Toll Revised to 173* (media release). Available at: www.police.vic.gov.au/content.asp?Document_ID=20350 (accessed 31 March 2014).

VietNamNews (2013) 'PM Agrees to Expand Support for Families Threatened by Floods'. Available at: http://english.vietnamnet.vn/fms/government/70999/pm-agrees-to-expand-support-for-families-threatened-by-floods.html (accessed 31 October 2013).

World Bank (2012) 'World Bank Indicators – Bangladesh – Rural Population'. Available at: www.tradingeconomics.com/bangladesh/rural-population-percent-of-total-population-wb-data.html (accessed 11 November 2013).

World Vision (2010) *Typhoon Ketsana: One Year Anniversary*. Hanoi: World Vision Vietnam.

Index